SOLUTIONS

CHARLES DARWIN
and the Theory of Natural Selection

BY RENEE SKELTON

Illustrated by Jim Robinson

BARRON'S

NEW YORK • LONDON • TORONTO • SYDNEY

First edition published 1987
by Barron's Educational Series, Inc.

© Copyright 1987 by Eisen, Durwood & Co., Inc.
Cover art by Daniel Maffia
Illustrated by Jim Robinson

All inquiries should be addressed to:
Barron's Educational Series, Inc.
250 Wireless Blvd.
Hauppauge, NY 11788

Library of Congress Catalog Card No. 87-19564

International Standard Book No. 0-8120-3923-8

Library of Congress Cataloging-in-Publication Data

Skelton, Renee.
Charles Darwin and the theory of natural selection.

(Solutions)
Bibliography.
Includes index.
Summary: Traces the life of the English naturalist from his
early years through his expedition aboard the H.M.S. Beagle
and the development of his theory of evolution by natural
selection.
 1. Darwin, Charles, 1809-1882 — Juvenile literature.
2. Natural selection — Juvenile literature. 3. Evolution —
Juvenile literature. 4. Naturalists — England — Biography —
Juvenile literature. [1. Darwin, Charles, 1809-1882.
2. Naturalists. 3. Evolution. 4. Natural selection]
I. Robinson, Jim, ill. II. Title. III. Series.
QH31.D2.S58   1987   575.01'62 [92]   87-19564
ISBN 0-8120-3923-8

Printed in the United States of America
789 9693 987654321

CONTENTS

CONTENTS

What sort of person does it take to change science forever? In Charles Darwin's case, it took a determined young man. He stuck with an idea for more than twenty years to prove he was right—even when everyone around him said he was wrong!

From the time that Charles was a boy, he loved the outdoors. He loved to hike through woods or stroll in gardens. He collected plants, insects, rocks and birds' eggs. He wondered about the many kinds of plants and animals he saw around him. Where did they come from? How did each one of them live?

Young Charles Darwin dreamed of visiting faraway places and seeing exotic plant and animal life. When Darwin was twenty-two, he got that chance. He took a five-year voyage around the world, and worked as a naturalist. On the trip, he saw, collected, and studied many new forms of life. He also uncovered a number of strange things that raised questions in his mind.

Most scientists believed that living things did not change over time. But as Darwin traveled, he became convinced that living things had changed during earth's long history.

How did life on earth develop? Had it changed since Creation? Darwin wanted to know. He thought about these questions for most of his life. He worked hard to find the answers. Finally, he published his idea of the truth: an amazing book called *On The Origin of Species*. In it, he explained his theory of evolution by natural selection. His theory states that over millions of years all forms of life on earth have changed. They began as different plants and animals than the ones we see today. This idea did not start with Darwin. It had been around for a long time. But almost no one believed it. After Darwin made his case, though, people could no longer say that evolution was a crazy idea. Darwin collected information for more than twenty years to substantiate the theory of evolution. He also came up with his own theory—natural selection—to show how evolution worked.

Because of his ideas, Charles Darwin's work is important to natural science. But Darwin's life is an important example, too. He overcame a lot to do his important work. As a child, Darwin was always at odds with the adults around him. He didn't do well in school and couldn't seem to settle on a career. He liked collecting things and studying nature. But no one else saw any value in it. They wanted him to give it up and concentrate on something more useful. Darwin wouldn't give up. He stuck with his hobby and made it his career.

In his later life, Darwin overcame other obstacles. He became ill after his voyage around the world. Hardly a day passed without pain. Often after a short stroll in his garden, he would have to lie down and rest. But Darwin kept going. He worked on his scientific theories though at times he could not leave his house.

Charles Darwin is a person worth getting to know

for his ideas about life and science. But he is also worth knowing because of his stubborn mind! He stuck to what he believed in and went forward even in hard times.

If Darwin were alive today, he might be surprised that his theory is still being talked about—and questioned. People still argue about the meaning of evolution through natural selection, and even about whether or not Darwin's theory should be taught in school. More than one hundred years after his death, Charles Darwin still affects the way we all think about life on earth.

CHAPTER ONE

Darwin's Early Years

Rows of rocks—some shiny and black, others marbled with bands of color. Some with flecks that looked like dots of silver and gold. Beautiful white, gold, and brown butterflies with delicate wings. These were the toys of Charles Darwin. He loved to collect things, watch them, pull them apart, and see how they worked. He spent hours in the woods and gardens near his home in Shrewsbury, England, picking up anything new and interesting. Then he would return home, his pockets bulging with treasures.

Charles's family couldn't understand why he would want to collect these things. It all seemed like such a waste of time. So much effort to collect a lot of trash. But Charles didn't see it that way. As he wandered along, his sharp eyes would spot a glittering rock, or a brightly colored leaf. He'd scoop it up and whisk it away to his room to become part of his collection.

As Charles Darwin walked through the woods near home, he could never have guessed that his collection was giving him a great education. He certainly never thought that it might ever lead to anything important. He would

1

Darwin - Age 6

SHREWSBURY

have been shocked to know that more than a century after his death, people still remember his name.

Charles Darwin was a lucky boy in many ways. The Darwin family was wealthy. Young Charles had everything that he could ever want. His family name had the power to help him win a place in society.

Charles's grandfather, Erasmus Darwin, had been a doctor and a famous poet. He was highly respected, too. King George III—the English king against whom American colonists had fought—asked Erasmus to join his medical staff. But Erasmus was brave enough to turn the king down.

Charles's father, Robert Waring Darwin, was a doctor too. He was one of the busiest doctors in Shrewsbury.

MOUNT HOUSE

Dr. Darwin was a huge man—six feet, two inches tall and more than three hundred pounds. He loved his children, but was very strict with them. Often, after dinner, he would sit and talk to them for hours about the right way to behave.

Charles's mother, Susannah, was a member of the wealthy Wedgwood family. The Wedgwoods owned a business that made pottery and china. Valuable Wedgwood china is still made today.

Susannah Darwin died in July of 1817, when Charles was only eight years old. His sisters were so sad and shocked that they hardly spoke of her after her death. Later, Charles wrote that he remembered little of his mother, except the dark dressing gown she wore when she was dying and the writing table she kept near her bed. Strangely, most other memories of her faded.

The Darwin family owned Mount House in Shrewsbury. It was a large, three-story home on a hill over-looking the Severn River. The house was a busy place. Charles, his father, four sisters, a brother and the family servants kept it that way.

After Charles's mother died, he was raised by his father and his sister Caroline. Caroline was nine years older than Charles. She took on most of the job of looking after him. She even taught him at home before he was sent to school.

Like most young children, Charles got into his share of trouble. He was a real pest to Caroline. Whenever he entered a room and saw Caroline, he would think, "I wonder what she will blame me for this time?"

Charles's relationship with his father was smoother—at least in the beginning. Charles loved and respected his father. He enjoyed being with him and sometimes would go along with Dr. Darwin as he called on patients. But Charles was afraid of his father, too. He could be bossy—and Charles had a hard time pleasing him.

Dr. Darwin had great plans for Charles. It was true that Charles would never have to work to earn his living. He would inherit enough money from Dr. Darwin to live well for the rest of his life. But Dr. Darwin believed that every man should do some type of useful work. And he knew just the type of work he wanted Charles to do. Dr. Darwin and *his* father had both studied medicine at Edinburgh University in Scotland. He wanted both of his sons, Erasmus and Charles, to do the same. That way, his sons could become useful and respected men in

Shrewsbury. What was the problem? Dr. Darwin's idea of what Charles should do with his life and Charles's idea were very different.

The first step in turning Charles into the right kind of young man was to get him an education. Shortly after his mother died, Dr. Darwin sent Charles to a day school run by a Unitarian minister. A year later, at age nine, Charles entered the Shrewsbury School, a boys' school run by Dr. Samuel Butler.

The Shrewsbury School was only about a mile from the Darwin home, but Charles lived at school with the other boys. Still, he loved to run home and visit his family after classes. Charles would usually poke around his room for some item, or stay a little too long, playing with one of his sisters or his brother. Then he would have to scoot back to school in a hurry. Often, he would arrive just in time to slip in before the doors were locked for the night.

School was tough for Charles. The fact is, he really hated it. "School, . . . to me, was simply a blank," he wrote later.

Of course, school in Charles Darwin's day was very different from school today. He studied Greek, Latin, math, ancient history, classic books, and poetry. There were no art, gym, or music classes. Students couldn't take wood shop or join the computer club. They had to sit up straight in hard wooden chairs and listen to their teachers. Silently, they copied down what was said. For some subjects, they would have to learn their lessons by heart. Then they would have to stand up and recite them in front of the whole class.

Charles wasn't good at languages. He found ancient history boring. He also hated to learn poetry by heart. He would usually practice his poem in chapel right before class. Right after class, he would just as quickly forget it. When Charles had to write poetry, he would find old poems in books. Then he would put different lines of them together, to make a new poem that he could pass off as his own.

Because school bored him, Charles didn't do well there. Sometimes he tried, but he didn't really care. He never did better than average. Charles's fair to poor grades made his teachers sure that he just wasn't very smart. His father didn't think he was smart either. After all, Charles had done nothing to prove that he was. Dr. Darwin was very disappointed in his son.

Charles's father and teachers didn't know it, but Charles had a good mind and really did love to learn. He just didn't want to learn the subjects he was being taught in school. Charles hardly opened his Latin and math books. But on his own, he loved to read books about nature and trips to faraway places. He could sit for hours, too, and read the plays of Shakespeare.

Charles did do well in some things. They just were not valued by the people around him. He loved to take walks in the woods and gardens around Shrewsbury. He would watch the plants, animals, and insects around him. He saw birds nesting, and insects feeding on the flowers. He could name many of them and talk about their habits. But instead of asking Charles about how a robin's egg

Josiah Wedgwood II

DEVONPORT

was different than the egg of a wren, his teachers always asked him to recite poems and speak Greek!

Charles also loved to ride horses and hunt game birds. He became an expert at both. When he was older, Charles once found a dying bird that he had shot a day before. It still lay, weak and wounded, in the meadow where it had fallen. Charles was very upset that he alone had hurt the bird. So he made up his mind that he would never shoot birds again, except for food or for scientific collecting. But while he was young he loved to hunt. As a teenager, Charles spent hunting season at Maer, the country home of his Uncle Josiah Wedgwood.

Charles also loved chemistry, although it wasn't taught at the Shrewsbury School. He got his hands on a chemistry book and read it cover to cover. His brother, Erasmus, had set up a little laboratory in the family toolshed. Charles loved to hang around and help him

7

perform his experiments. The two young chemists often worked late into the night.

Somehow, word spread at school that Charles was doing chemistry experiments with his brother. Some of his classmates made fun of him for spending his time on chemistry. They even nicknamed him "gas." Headmaster Butler was not pleased. Dr. Butler thought Charles's chemistry experiments and his collections were a foolish waste of time, especially for a boy who did so poorly in his studies.

Charles's father was not pleased either. He didn't understand how nature walks or butterfly collections or chemistry experiments were going to help Charles start a career. Charles's father once told him angrily, "You care for nothing but shooting, dogs and rat-catching, and you will be a disgrace to yourself and all your family."

Charles was hurt by his father's scolding. He wanted to please his father. But Charles was also very stubborn about some things. He knew what he enjoyed and what he did not. He would try to find a career, as his father wanted. But all the teasing and talk of those around him could not convince Charles Darwin to give up his "useless" hobbies.

College Days

At the age of 16, Charles was still studying at the Shrewsbury School. But he continued to get poor grades, and complained that he was bored. His father decided that a change was needed. So in October, 1825, Dr. Darwin took Charles out of Shrewsbury. He wanted Charles to get serious. It was time for Charles to find some career.

There were a number of acceptable careers for a wealthy young gentleman. He could become a doctor. He could also study law. Or he could become an officer in the army. But Charles really didn't have much of a choice in the matter. His father had decided that Charles should become a doctor. So late in 1825, Dr. Darwin sent Charles to Edinburgh University in Scotland, where his brother Erasmus was already in medical school.

It didn't take Charles long to find out that medical school was not the place for him. Because he had not done well at the Shrewsbury School, he was behind many of his classmates. Charles hated medical school so much that he didn't try really hard to catch up.

On cold winter mornings, Charles would drag himself out of bed to get ready for his 8:00 AM classes. He was glad that he could finally take chemistry. But his other classes were so boring, he said, that they were "fearful to remember." His anatomy teacher made his classes, "as dull as he was himself, and the subject disgusted me."

Not only did Charles find his classes dull, he found dealing with ill people very hard. Charles had to visit hospitals to learn about the patients and their diseases. Many of the illnesses were hard for him to watch and study.

Watching operations was also part of a doctor's training. In the early 1800's, operations were frightening. Patients were not given drugs to numb them or put them to sleep. During surgery, patients were strapped down but wide awake. There was a lot of blood and even more screaming. Charles just couldn't take it. He couldn't stand to see blood. Charles almost felt the patients' pain himself. He did watch two operations as a student. But before either of them was completed, he ran out of the operating room. To Charles, the operating room looked like a torture chamber. "The two cases haunted me for many a year," he later wrote.

Charles promised himself that he would never view an operation gain. He kept his promise. But of course, he realized that this was a real problem for a medical student. How could he learn to treat patients if he couldn't even watch surgery? Charles stayed in medical school mainly to please his father. He was afraid to say that he wanted to quit. But he knew that he never could or would become a doctor.

Although Charles continued to attend classes at Edinburgh, he was just going through the motions. He did just enough to get by. That is not to say Charles wasn't learning. He learned quite a bit—*outside* of class.

Charles's early interest in studying nature had not left him. He still loved collecting insects, rocks, and other things. He was forced to put aside these hobbies for the sake of school. But he found ways to keep his interest in natural science alive.

Charles joined several nature clubs, such as the Plinian Society. He went to their evening meetings in his spare time. There he heard famous scientists—like John J. Audubon—speak, read, and discuss their work.

Through the science clubs, Charles also met many professional nature scientists. He made friends with one of them. Dr. Robert Grant was a marine zoologist, a scientist who studies sea animals. Dr. Grant took Charles on trips to the coast of Scotland. There, they would wander along the shore, collecting small sea animals from tidal pools. Charles would bring some of the little creatures back to his room to study. He would look at them closely and sometimes cut apart, or dissect them.

Charles also liked to visit the fishermen at Newhaven, a nearby fishing village. He would help them catch oysters in the local bay, called the Firth of Forth. Then he would take home some of the specimens he caught, for his own studies.

There was a black taxidermist living in Edinburgh at the time. (Taxidermy is the science of skinning and stuffing animals.) Charles took lessons from him in skinning and stuffing birds. Charles would often sit with the man, listening to his tales of travels to faraway places.

Charles was not learning much about medicine. But he *was* learning more and more about nature.

Charles also liked to enjoy himself like any other young gentleman. He and his friends were members of the Glutton Club. The club met each week for huge dinners. Then the members would drink wine, listen to music, and play cards.

Summers were free, pleasant times for Charles. He could stay outdoors all day. He spent some of his summer vacations with friends, hiking through the countryside. On a trip through northern Wales, Charles and his group walked thirty miles a day, carrying their belongings in backpacks.

Autumn, before the start of school, was time for bird hunting. Charles loved to return to his Uncle Josiah's estate. He would ride and hunt from sunup to sundown. He would leave his clothes laid out and his shoes unlaced near his bed. That way, he could slip into them as soon as he woke up in the morning. He didn't want to waste a minute of precious hunting time.

In the evenings, the family would gather in the garden behind the house. There they would eat, talk, and listen to music. Later in life, Charles looked back on these fall evenings at Maer as some of the most pleasant times of his life.

Back at medical school, life was not as pleasant. Charles was still doing poorly. He was afraid to tell his father the truth—that he didn't want to be a doctor. But, in letters home, he did pour out his feelings to one of his sisters. Word got back to Dr. Darwin that Charles was miserable. Fortunately for Charles, his father finally accepted the truth. His son would never become a doctor. So he brought Charles home to Shrewsbury to decide what to do next.

Dr. Darwin was very disappointed. But he didn't give up on Charles. He came up with another idea for his son's career. He told Charles he could go to Cambridge University and become a minister.

This would not have been Charles's first choice as a career. He agreed to think about it. After all, he didn't have any idea of what kind of job he would like to do. He loved natural science, but he couldn't make a good living in that field. At least that is what everyone told him. Being a minister might not be so bad. He had been raised as a member of the Church of England. He believed in the Bible. Besides, his father would leave him enough money to live comfortably for the rest of his life. So the small salary of a minister would not be a problem.

It might be especially nice, Charles thought, if he got a country parish. Then he would be able to continue his nature studies and build his collection. In fact, for the first time, his hobbies might be easily accepted. After all, nature is God's creation. So it would be fine for a minister to study nature.

But there was a problem to solve first. During his two years at medical school, Charles had forgotten the classics, such as Latin. He would need these to become a minister. Charles had to work for a few months with a private tutor at Shrewsbury to brush up before he could enter Cambridge. Then in 1828, at the age of nineteen,

Charles began his studies at Christ's College, Cambridge. He studied classics, religion, and mathematics.

Charles told himself that studying religion was a good idea. He would please his family, and especially his father. But he wasn't really interested in the ministry. Again, it showed in his work at school. He just couldn't get excited about his classes. The idea of becoming a minister didn't appeal to him as much as he had thought it might. Later, Charles would write that his three years at Cambridge were wasted.

As usual, Charles saved his energy for his hobbies. He worked hard on his collection. At Cambridge, beetles became his favorite. There were so many sizes, shapes, and colors. Some were beautiful to Charles. Some looked scary. But he was always on the lookout for a kind of beetle he had not seen before. When he saw a new kind, Charles just *had* to have it.

One day, while searching for new beetles, Charles tore some bark from a tree trunk. Two rare beetles fell out. Charles wanted both of them. So he reached out and grabbed one in each hand. Just then, another rare beetle raced in front of him. Charles got so excited, he didn't know what to do. Without thinking, he popped one of the beetles he was holding into his mouth. He scooped up the third with his free hand. All of a sudden, Charles felt a stinging in his mouth. He jumped up, spitting out the bug in his mouth and dropping the other two. Charles was shocked. He would never try *that* again.

Charles's friends at Cambridge became a big part of his life. They found him warm, generous, and fun loving.

John Henslow

CHRIST'S COLLEGE

Most of his pals were young and wealthy like himself. He enjoyed their company even if they were, as he later said, "low-minded." They all loved to ride horses. They enjoyed hunting, gambling, and eating good meals together. There was much singing, card-playing, and playing practical jokes.

At Cambridge, Charles also made friends with two members of the faculty. One of these friendships would change his life.

John Henslow was a minister at Cambridge. He also taught botany, the study of plant life. He was in his thirties and got along well with his young students. Henslow held a weekly open house for students interested in botany. Charles's course of study didn't include botany classes, but he was very interested in the subject. So when Charles found out that he could go to the open houses, he did.

Charles quickly attracted Henslow's attention. The professor found Charles pleasant, bright, and interesting. He took Charles under his wing and encouraged his interest in natural science. Henslow and Charles Darwin became good friends. They would often take long walks and talk. On the walks, Charles would help Henslow collect plant specimens. Charles learned many new plant names, and Henslow taught him a lot about botany, too. Charles was with Henslow so often that some of the students at school started calling Charles, "The man who walks with Henslow."

In Henslow, Charles had finally found an adult who encouraged his interest in natural science. Henslow told Charles that he *could* make a career in natural science—if he worked at it. Charles wanted to try, but he knew that his father would be against it. He couldn't believe that his hobby could ever become his career. Soon, a letter would change Charles's mind about that. In fact, that letter would change Charles's whole life.

CHAPTER THREE

Travel Plans

As he continued his work at Cambridge, Charles also kept reading about nature. In the winter of 1830, he read an exciting book by the German explorer Alexander von Humboldt. The book was called *A Personal Narrative of Travels to the Equinoctial Regions of America During the Years 1700–1804.* In the book, Humboldt described his adventure in the Canary Islands and the tropics of North and South America. He also described many new kinds, or species, of animals and plants that he had seen along the way. For a collector like Charles, a trip such as von Humboldt's seemed like paradise.

Von Humboldt's book "stirred up in me a burning zeal to add even the most humble contribution to natural science," Charles wrote later.

Charles dreamed of traveling to exotic places. He told some of his friends that he was going to visit the Canary Islands. There, he would explore the rain forest just like von Humboldt. He hoped that a group of his friends would come with him. It would be such a wonderful adventure.

While Charles was dreaming of adventures, he managed to graduate from Cambridge. That is, he just barely graduated. He still had to stay a few extra months to finish some requirements. But finally, in 1831, he got his Bachelor of Arts degree in theology. He ranked tenth among those who graduated without honors.

On one of Charles's many trips to John Henslow's house, he met Professor Adam Sedgwick. Sedgwick was head of the geology department at Cambridge. Charles became friends with Sedgwick, too. Sedgwick had made Charles curious about geology. In August 1831, Charles went with Sedgwick on a trip to North Wales. He taught Charles how to name and recognize rocks and minerals. He explained why and how certain rock formations came to be. He also taught Charles how to collect rock specimens. It was Charles's first experience in field geology—and it would come in handy in the future. But fall hunting season would be starting soon. So Charles left Wales to get to his Uncle Josiah's estate by September 1.

On his way to Maer, Charles stopped at home in Shrewsbury. A letter from John Henslow was waiting for him there. Henslow's letter contained exciting news. A royal ship, the HMS *Beagle*, would soon leave for a two-year voyage around the world. The trip's main goal would be to map the coast of southern South America. But the captain, Robert Fitzroy, wanted a young gentleman to go along as naturalist and companion. The naturalist would share the captain's cabin and meals. He would study nature wherever the ship docked and collect specimens of the plants and animals. There would be no pay. In fact, the naturalist would have to pay his own way aboard the ship. But that would be no problem for a wealthy young man like Charles Darwin.

Henslow had been asked to take the job himself. But his wife did not want him away from home for so long a period of time. So Henslow suggested Charles. He wrote to him:

"I have stated that I consider you to be the best qualified person I know . . . qualified for collecting, observing, and noting anything worthy . . ."

Charles was delighted. What a chance for an adventure. A trip around the world, and as a naturalist! Finally, a way he might use his knowledge of nature and his love of collecting for something important.

Of course, it was too early to celebrate yet. First Charles needed his father's permission to go on the voyage. After all, Dr. Darwin was supporting him. He would have to pay Charles's way aboard the ship.

Charles was nervous about asking his father. Finally, he put the question to him. Would his father permit him to sign on as the *Beagle*'s naturalist and sail around the world? Dr. Darwin couldn't believe what Charles was asking. Charles had never been interested in school. He had done very poorly. He had been sent to medical school and had dropped out. He had just graduated from college as a minister. Finally, he could enter a profession. Now, it seemed, he wanted to throw that away, too, and for what? Some wild scheme of sailing around the world to

19

look at trees and collect animal bones! Dr. Darwin was very upset. He said no. Absolutely, positively, no.

Charles was crushed. He pleaded with his father to change his mind. He tried all sorts of arguments. Nothing worked. Dr. Darwin grew tired of the whole matter. Finally, he said something that he hoped would end the discussion. He told Charles that if he could find one man of common sense who would advise him to go on the journey, he would grant permission.

Charles didn't think that there was the slightest chance of finding such a person. He would have to pass up the trip. He decided to forget about the whole matter for a while, and he left to go hunting at his Uncle Josiah's estate.

When Charles got to Maer, he told the whole story to the Wedgwoods. They could see how very upset Charles was and they felt sorry for him. Their reaction was completely different than Charles's father's had been. They thought Dr. Darwin was wrong to keep Charles from going on the trip. They told Charles that the *Beagle* voyage would be educational and exciting. They thought it was a once-in-a-lifetime chance. They didn't believe that Charles should pass this up.

The day after Charles arrived at Maer, his Uncle Josiah rode with him back to the Darwin home in Shrewsbury. Josiah Wedgwood wanted to speak with Dr. Darwin personally on his young nephew's behalf. He told Charles's father that he thought Charles should be allowed to go on the trip. Then he gave his reasons.

Dr. Darwin greatly respected Josiah Wedgwood's

opinion. Charles reminded him of what he had said earlier. If one man with common sense advised Charles to go on the trip, he would give his permission. Josiah Wedgwood was certainly a man with common sense. Dr. Darwin kept his word. Yes, Charles could go on his trip around the world on the *Beagle*.

Dr. Darwin had said Charles could go, but he still had his doubts. To make his father feel better, Charles told him that going on board ship would save money. At school, Charles had always overspent his allowance. Charles told his father that he would have to be pretty clever to overspend his allowance on a ship. Charles's father looked at his son and said, with a slight smile, "Yes, but they say you are very clever."

Now that Dr. Darwin had said yes, Charles was almost on his way. Still, before he was sure of going on the trip there was one more big thing to do.

Charles had to meet the captain of the *Beagle*, Robert Fitzroy. Captain Fitzroy would make the final choice. Charles was nervous about meeting Fitzroy. First, he knew that other men had been asked. What if one of them already had gotten the job? Even if no one had gotten it, would Fitzroy like him? If he did not impress Fitzroy, the trip would be off.

Fitzroy was very stern and religious. One of the reasons he wanted to go on the trip was to set up a Christian mission on Tierra del Fuego, the island at the southern tip of South America. Fitzroy had gone to Tierra del Fuego on an earlier trip. His party had captured four natives as ransom for a stolen boat. Fitzroy had brought the

four to England. One had died. He had the other three
educated and converted to Christianity. Now he wanted
to return them to Tierra del Fuego to spread Christianity
among their people.

Taking a naturalist along was not unusual for English
ships. Naturalists often brought back valuable information about foreign lands. But Fitzroy also had a religious
reason for wanting a naturalist with him. He wanted the
naturalist to find proof that what happened in the Bible's
book of Genesis was true, word for word.

Charles's meeting with Captain Fitzroy took place
on September 5, 1831. It was a good meeting. Darwin
and Fitzroy were both young. Charles was twenty-two,
Fitzroy twenty-six. Darwin later described him as a hand-
some man with the manners of a gentleman. He talked
with Charles about his family, his education, and his be-
liefs. He also warned Charles about the possible dangers

of the voyage. Nothing Fitzroy said lessened Charles's excitement.

There was one more thing that the captain cared about. That was, oddly enough, the way Charles looked. Fitzroy believed that someone's eyes, nose, and mouth could tell what that person was like. Unfortunately for Charles, he had a small, rounded nose. To Captain Fitzroy, that meant that Charles was a man who would be lazy or dishonest.

If the captain had gone by that alone, Charles Darwin would never have sailed on the *Beagle*. But Charles made a good impression on the captain. He saw that Charles knew a lot about nature. So, ignoring Charles's nose, Captain Fitzroy gave him the job.

Charles was thrilled. He started preparing for the trip. He bought a supply of clothing. He stocked up on notebooks to record everything he would see. He bought a microscope, a telescope with a compass, a magnet, geological tools, and materials for preserving specimens. He also bought two pistols and a rifle for protection, and to hunt animals to send back to England for study. And of course he brought many books for the weeks at sea.

As ship's naturalist, Charles would not have much to do while the ship sailed the ocean. He would catch some sea life in nets. But he would be most busy on land. His job would be to collect plants, insects, and other animals that lived where the *Beagle* visited. He would also collect rocks, and describe the landscape of each area. Charles could study some of his finds in his small lab area on the *Beagle*. But most of them would be crated and sent to England for later study. John Henslow agreed to accept most of the crates as Charles sent them. He promised to store them until Charles returned home to sort the material.

After gathering supplies for the trip, Charles arrived in Plymouth, England, on October 24, 1831. He stayed there almost two months while the *Beagle* was readied for the voyage. During most of this time, Darwin had terrible headaches. He wanted to go on the trip. But he was very nervous. The months he spent waiting at Plymouth gave him plenty of time to think, and to worry about everything that might go wrong.

Sailing in Darwin's day was often dangerous. On its previous voyage, the *Beagle* had lost quite a few of its crew members. Some had been swept overboard in angry seas. Some had gotten sick and had died along the way. One man killed himself. Darwin had a lot to think about.

But finally, on December 27, 1831, the waiting ended. The *Beagle* sailed from Devonport, England. The trip was to last two years. But Charles would not see home again for five.

At the end of the trip, Charles's intention was to start again where he had left off. He would give up wandering. He would settle down to the life of a minister. Charles had no way of knowing that the voyage would make it impossible for him to do so. He would come back five years later, a new and different man.

CHAPTER FOUR

From England to Brazil

The *Beagle* was a kind of sailboat called a brig. It had ten large guns. But on this voyage these guns were not to be used. The *Beagle*'s mission was to collect information, not to fight battles. The crew was to map the coast of southern South America and nearby islands. After this, the *Beagle* would cross the Pacific and Indian oceans, sail around the southern tip of Africa, then head north through the Atlantic and return to England.

The *Beagle* had a crew of 74 men. Besides the captain, crew, and naturalist Darwin, the ship carried an artist, an instrument-maker and Fitzroy's personal servant.

Charles hired Sims Covington, a cabin boy, to be his servant. He called Sims "an odd sort of person," but Sims was very useful. Charles taught Sims taxidermy, so that he could help Charles collect and prepare specimens. The two became friends and Sims stayed with Darwin for years after they returned to England.

When the voyage began, Charles wondered what kind of choice he had made. The *Beagle* was a very uncomfortable home. Charles had to share a tiny cabin with the captain, another officer, and lots of equipment. The cabin was very cramped. Charles's bed was little more than a hammock. He could not even stretch out on it completely. Soon, he found the only way he *could* stretch out. He removed the drawers from a cabinet at the foot of his bed, and stuck his feet through the holes where the drawers had been.

Charles had never been to sea before, and he did not get off to a good start. The wintry Atlantic was cold and rough. Charles's cabin was in the rear of the *Beagle*. That part of the ship tossed and rocked the most. During the first couple of weeks, the *Beagle* rolled on the stormy Atlantic. Charles became very seasick. He spent a lot of his time on his bed eating raisins.

Charles also had a lot of time to get to know the captain. After all, he slept and ate with him. He greatly respected Fitzroy's ability as a leader and a seaman. He found Fitzroy intelligent and hardworking. All of the men did. But they were also a bit afraid of Fitzroy. He was moody and had quite a bad temper when things did not suit him. He could be quite the gentleman, but the crew learned to stay away from him at certain times—such as early in the morning. That is when he would walk the ship looking for anything that was not in order. If he found it, heaven help the person responsible.

Most of the time, Fitzroy and Darwin got along fairly well. In fact, Fitzroy wrote of Charles,

Darwin is a very sensible, hard-working man, and a very pleasant messmate. I never saw a shore-going fellow come into the ways of a ship as thoroughly as Darwin . . .

Still, there was not a lot for Charles to do aboard ship. When he could, he would read. One of the books he had brought on board was called *Principles of Geology*. It was written by Charles Lyell. Lyell had come up with many new ideas about how the earth's surface had formed. Lyell's ideas were very different from those of other earth scientists, or geologists.

Other geologists thought that changes in the earth's surface were caused only by acts of God. One such act was the great flood described in the Bible. The flood waters could have caused many changes in the earth's surface. Otherwise, most geologists believed that earth's surface was exactly as God had created it.

Lyell did not agree. He thought that earth's surface was always changing. Some changes came from great, sudden events, such as the flood of the Bible or the shaking of an earthquake. But the earth also showed smaller changes, like the way the wind and water ate away, or eroded the land. Over millions of years, even these gradual changes could cause a great difference in the look of earth's surface.

John Henslow had given Lyell's book to Charles. Charles didn't know what to think of the Lyell book at first. But he did find Lyell's ideas interesting. During his travels in South America, he would see evidence that Lyell's ideas were often quite sound. They would play a great part in Charles's thinking about how the earth and its creatures had developed.

On January 16, 1832, Charles finally set his feet again on land. It was on the island of Sao Tiago, part of the Cape Verde Islands near Africa's northwest coast.

The heat was scorching and the landscape was none too inviting. But Charles was delighted to be exploring new territory at last. After all, this was his first trip to the tropics. He was seeing many strange plants and animals for the first time. He was especially thrilled to see his first coconut tree up close.

Charles explored the island on horseback. At times, a black clergyman was his guide. As he traveled, Charles observed the weather, the plants, the animals, and the customs of the people on the island. Charles saw everything, and as he traveled he constantly scribbled his thoughts in the notebooks he carried with him.

Darwin stayed on Sao Tiago for twenty-three days. While he was there, he found the first hint that Charles Lyell's wild ideas might not be so wild after all. While exploring the coast, Darwin came upon a cliff. High up on the cliff, he saw a band of white rock. It ran along the cliff for several miles. Charles wanted to get a closer look. So he picked his way carefully along a rocky path to get nearer. When he did, he saw that the white rock was made of tiny seashells. Charles wondered how this could be. The rock layer was high above the level of the ocean. How in the world did seashells get way up there?

Darwin thought and thought, but he could come to only one conclusion. That white band of seashells was once under the sea. Something had lifted it up to where it stood now. If it happened little by little, that would support Lyell's theory that the earth's surface is shaped by many gradual changes. But it would take much more evidence for Charles to come to this conclusion.

In mid-February 1832 the *Beagle* set sail again. The ship headed 1500 miles across the Atlantic to the coast of South America. The *Beagle* would spend three and a half years sailing up and down the South American coast. The *Beagle* would take Darwin to shore from time to time. He would often spend weeks on hikes through the countryside. He climbed mountains, paddled up and down rivers, and hiked through jungles. He rode on horseback over plains and deserts. On the way he would collect plants and rocks, study the landscape, and take notes on the people he met. Often Charles would stop at houses or ranches in the wilderness and ask for shelter for the night. At other times, he would camp out in the open.

While Darwin was doing his work on shore, the *Beagle* and its crew would sail along the coast. They would map the coastline and nearby islands. The crew of the *Beagle* would then return to a port on the coast for rest, supplies—and to pick up Charles, the strange but likeable young man who was traveling with them. Then the ship would sail to its next stop.

On the way to South America, the *Beagle* crossed the equator. The sailors had an old tradition for those men crossing the equator for the first time. On this trip, it was Charles's turn. The playful crewmen blindfolded Charles, covered him with paint and tar, then shaved him

Voyage of the Beagle

1831   1836

Devonport

NORTH

RICA

Atlantic

Canary
Is.

Cape Verde
Is.

AFRIC

Galapagos Is.

Ocean

SOUTH

Callao

Bahia

AMERICA

Rio de Janeiro

Montevideo

Valparaiso

Around the World

Tierra
del
Fuego

Falkland Is.

0   1500 mls.
Scale

with a dull saw. Then he was thrown into a sail full of water. Darwin said he nearly drowned, but everyone, including Charles, laughed and had a good time.

The *Beagle* arrived on the coast of Brazil in late February 1832. The first stop was Bahia. Charles left the ship right away to take his first walk in the Brazilian rain forest. Darwin loved what he saw around him: "the elegance of the grasses, the novelty of the plants, the beauty of the flowers, the glossy green of the bushes. . . ." The plants were so thick in the forest, he wrote, that the leaves high overhead blocked out the sun completely. The forest floor lay in deep shade and silence.

The *Beagle* sailed from Bahia on March 18 and reached Brazil's main city, Rio de Janeiro, on April 4. The *Beagle* then sailed back north to check its map readings. Darwin stayed behind. He rented space in a cottage on Botofogo Bay. He and the ship's artist, Augustus Earle, stayed there for three months. From the cottage, Darwin took several trips along the shore and deep into the forest.

A few days after he arrived, Charles set off with six others on a journey of one hundred miles. They were to visit the coffee plantation of a Mr. Patrick Lennon. Darwin wrote home:

It is an uncommon and most excellent opportunity and I shall see what has been so long my ambition, virgin forest uncut by man and tenanted by wild beasts. You will all be terrified at the thought of my combating with alligators and jaguars . . . [but] the expedition is really quite a safe one . . .

The trip through this part of the forest was a feast of new sights, sounds, and smells. All sorts of animals could be seen through the treetops—swinging monkeys, brightly-colored parrots and butterflies. Amazing insects and snakes crawled along tree trunks, through leaves and branches on the forest floor. The forest was thick and dark. Its huge trees had branches that met hundreds of feet overhead. Darwin dined on freshly-picked oranges and ripe bananas. And as he walked, the air was full of the wonderful smell of pepper, cinnamon, and clove.

Darwin collected as he traveled. He studied the many types of plants and animals in the rain forest. He also spent a lot of time just watching animals and insects as they built homes, caught food, and moved from place to place. Many of the animals seemed to spend their whole lives in the trees—or perhaps just one tree. Darwin began to realize that no matter how small or strange, some form of life was suited to every kind of environment. Charles was learning a lot about the many ways that living things survive.

As they traveled, Charles and his party often stayed at inns, called *vendas*. These inns were very rough. Sometimes they had openings in the walls for windows, and dirt floors. Charles complained that the inns and their keepers were often filthy. He and his party were treated rudely and had to wait hours for a poor meal. "It not infrequently happened, that we were obliged to kill, with stones, the poultry for our own supper," Charles wrote. When supper did come, no knives, forks or spoons came with it.

While Charles was visiting Brazil, he studied the lives of the black people there. Many Africans had been brought to Brazil to work as slaves. Charles saw how hard the blacks had to work on the farms and in the cities he visited. They were often treated cruelly. Charles hated slavery. He hated the idea that one man could own and mistreat another. Later he put his feelings down on paper:

Near Rio de Janeiro I lived opposite to an old lady, who kept screws to crush the fingers of her female slaves. I have stayed in a house where a young household mulatto, daily and hourly, was . . . beaten enough to break the spirit of the lowest animal. I have seen a little boy, six or seven years old, struck with a horsewhip . . . on his naked head, for having handed me a glass of water not quite clean. . . . And these deeds are done . . . by men, who profess to . . . believe in God . . . It makes one's blood boil . . . to think that we Englishmen and our American descendents, with their boastful cries of liberty, have been and are so guilty . . .

When Charles got back to the *Beagle*, he talked to Fitzroy about what he had seen. This included slavery. Fitzroy saw nothing wrong with slavery, and he and Charles had a bitter argument about the subject. In fact, it was so bad, that Charles thought he might have to leave the ship. But when the captain's temper cooled, he sent for Charles and the two patched up their differences.

Charles and the captain didn't agree on a number of things, as it turned out. Charles learned that the best way to get along with Fitzroy was to keep his opinions to himself. As the trip continued, Charles's mind became full of new ideas about the development of the land and the life on it. Luckily, Fitzroy couldn't read Charles's mind.

CHAPTER FIVE

Argentina, Uruguay and Tierra del Fuego

C harles was getting used to a life of adventure. He was a friendly, easygoing young man who got along well with the sailors of the crew. Thin, six feet tall, and bearded, with bushy eyebrows and blue eyes, Darwin was a familiar figure as he moved around the ship. The crew members often joked about his strange job of collecting rocks, bones, and animal skins and wondered about the many books he read. They had nicknames for him: "philosopher" and "fly catcher."

One of the *Beagle*'s officers, a Lieutenant Wickham, teased Darwin about the many specimens he brought on board. He told Darwin, "If I were skipper, I would soon have you and all your damned mess out of the place!"

Darwin boarded the *Beagle* and sailed out of Rio de Janeiro on July 5, 1832. The *Beagle* sailed southwest along the coast of South America, mapping the coastline as it went. Charles spent much of his time watching the ocean life he could see from the *Beagle*'s deck. One day, he saw hundreds of porpoises. As they swam alongside the ship, they leaped gracefully out of the water.

Toward the end of July of 1832, the *Beagle* sailed into the wide, muddy mouth of the Rio de la Plata. First, the ship tried to land at Buenos Aires. But the Argentines fired a cannonball over the *Beagle*'s deck to keep it away. There had been a widespread outbreak of a killer disease, cholera, in England. The Argentines feared that the *Beagle* crew might be carrying the disease. The *Beagle* turned to the northern bank of the river. It dropped anchor in Montevideo, Uruguay, on July 26.

There was trouble at Montevideo when the *Beagle* arrived. Members of the Uruguayan army were about to revolt. The police chief begged Captain Fitzroy to send some men into town to keep order. Darwin and about thirty other men from the *Beagle* went into the city and marched up and down the streets with swords and pistols. The unruly soldiers disappeared.

The *Beagle* stayed at Montevideo for ten weeks. Darwin found a place in nearby Maldonado to pass the time. From there he would set off on trips into the countryside. Darwin saw huge flocks of ostriches. He once chased some on horseback to see how fast they could run. The ostriches won the race! Darwin also made a complete collection of the plants and animals of the area. In one morning, he collected eighty kinds of birds. He also added nine new kinds of snakes to his collection.

On his longer trips, Darwin often stayed in local homes overnight. Often, the local people found his customs as strange as he found theirs. "I carried with me some matches which I ignited by biting," he wrote. "It was thought so wonderful that a man should strike fire with his teeth, that [usually] the whole family [came] to see it . . ."

Darwin was delighted to be off on his own in another wild, new place. He wrote home:

Commonly I ride some few miles, [rest] my horse and start by some track into the . . . vegetation. Whilst seated in a tree, and eating my luncheon in the sublime solitude of the forest, the pleasure I experience is unspeakable.

By the middle of October 1832, the *Beagle* was ready to set sail again. The ship left the Rio de la Plata and headed south along the coast of Argentina. By December, the ship had reached Tierra del Fuego, the island at the southern tip of South America.

The *Beagle* came to the entrance of the Strait of Magellan on December 17, 1832. The strait separates the mainland of South America from Tierra del Fuego. Even in summer, the weather on this windswept island was cold and damp. Mist often blanketed the distant mountains. Charles described the island as covered by "one dense gloomy forest."

Charles was fascinated by the people of Tierra del Fuego. He was often cold, even though bundled up. But the Fuegians he saw simply wore shawls made of wild llama, or guanaco fur. These shawls offered no real protection from the wind and biting cold. Charles amazed that the natives could survive such cold. He began to compare them with the many animals he had seen. Both animals and people adapted to their environments— no matter how strange or forbidding the climate.

The *Beagle* made quite a long stop at Tierra del Fuego to return the three Fuegians and an English missionary, a Mr. Matthews, to the island. Darwin had a few days to explore while the ship was anchored at Good Success Bay. He found a mountainous land covered with a thick forest of trees. Because of the cold, the mountaintops were covered with caps of snow. As he walked, Darwin's feet sank into a thick pack of soggy, leaves and twigs. His way was often blocked by the trunks of huge, fallen, rotting trees. After climbing a mountain to collect plants, Darwin wrote:

The atmosphere here, with rain, hail and sleet, seems blacker than anywhere else. In the Strait of Magellan, the distant mountains appeared from their gloominess to lead beyond the confines of the world.

On December 21, the ship started on its way again. The next day, the *Beagle* began its trip around Cape Horn, the southern tip of Tierra del Fuego. The waters here were and are famous for their storminess. Sailing through these rough seas and howling winds, the *Beagle* made for a sheltered cove on the coast. The ship rode out the storm there. Then, on December 30, it set off again. Charles wrote:

The surf was breaking fearfully on the coast, and the

spray was carried 200 feet in height. On the 12th the gale was heavy and we did not know where we were. On the 13th the storm raged with its full fury. At noon a great sea broke over us. Had another sea followed the first, our fate would have been decided soon, and forever.

It took a whole month for the *Beagle* to pass safely around Tierra del Fuego. Then it headed eastward through the Strait of Magellan. Charles was terrified and seasick much of the time. He spent much of this part of the voyage below deck in his bed.

At the end of January 1833, they returned to Tierra del Fuego to help the Fuegians and the minister settle in their new home. Charles, Captain Fitzroy and some 27 other crew members left the *Beagle* in a few small boats. They followed a narrow creek, called Beagle Channel, which led toward the middle part of the island. There were several different tribes on the island. Along the way, Darwin and his party met many of them. The natives were always eager to trade or receive gifts. After a while, Darwin grew quite sick of them asking for so many gifts.

The *Beagle* crew members picked out a spot and built a crude house for the missionary and the Fuegians. They also planted gardens for them and left supplies.

Charles and the others continued for several more miles through Beagle Channel. On the way back a few days later, they stopped back at the newly built house and gardens. Both had been ruined by enemies among the native tribes. The English missionary was terrified and he went back on board the *Beagle* with Darwin and his party. The native Fuegians chose to stay behind.

The ship headed east through the Strait of Magellan. It continued north again, along the Atlantic coast of South America, to complete its mapping job. By July of 1833, the *Beagle* was back at the Rio de la Plata.

The *Beagle* would now follow its original route down the coast. The crew could double-check its readings. They could take more care with their maps and charts. And Charles would have time to explore Argentina more closely.

Charles had made a discovery about himself in the months since leaving Tierra del Fuego. He had definitely decided that this was the career he wanted. He wrote home to tell his family the news. If he could add to the world's knowledge of natural science, he wrote, he would be happy and satisfied with his life.

On July 24, the *Beagle* sailed from Maldonado for the second time. By August 3, it had reached the mouth of the Rio Negro in Argentina. Charles had been at sea long enough. He was anxious to get back on dry land and explore again. Charles asked Captain Fitzroy to leave him at Rio Negro. He knew that the *Beagle* would stop again at Bahia Blanca. Charles wanted to hike overland and meet the *Beagle* there. On the way, he could collect more plants and animals of the area. Captain Fitzroy agreed.

It took Darwin almost two weeks to reach Bahia Blanca. He made his trip with an English guide named

Argentine Gaucho

'Their politeness is excess-
ive... but whilst making
their graceful bows, they
seem quite ready...to cut
your throat.'

Mr. Harris, and five South American cowboys, or *gauchos*, who were all going in the same direction.

Not far from Rio Negro, he spotted flocks of flamingoes on a salt lake. But most of the trip crossed a hot, barren windswept area of the *pampas*, the grassy plain that covers most of northern Argentina. Charles did not find much interesting animal life to collect. He also didn't find many people. Still, he enjoyed the excitement of traveling to new places and learning new things.

There was good reason for the small population. Argentina was at war with the Indians who lived within its borders. The Indians had lived on the land for thousands of years. White settlers wanted the land for their homes, ranches and farms. General Juan de Rosas was in charge of getting the Indians out of their way. Argentine soldiers told Darwin that when they caught Indians, they killed all the men and women older than twenty, and sold young girls into slavery.

Charles thought it was terrible that the soldiers had killed so many of the natives. Villages of 2,000 to 3,000 people had been destroyed. The villagers were scattered. Many of them lived as *nomads*, or wanderers, on the plains. But Charles soon learned that the Indians could be as cruel as the settlers and soldiers. Charles's party had to be careful. If they met a large party of Indians, they might be attacked, or even killed.

Darwin found it helpful to be traveling with the gauchos. They knew the territory and were good at protecting themselves and those with them. They could be loyal friends but they were quite rough. Charles noted that many of them had scars on their faces—which proved that the knives they carried were often used. Charles respected the gauchos, but he feared them, too.

> They are tall, . . . handsome, . . . wear their moustaches, and long black hair curling down their backs. . . . Their politeness is excessive . . . but whilst making their graceful bows, they seem quite ready . . . to cut your throat.

Still, Darwin admired them. He wrote home and bragged to his family, "I have become quite a gaucho." He learned to sleep in the open air, smoke cigars, drink a strong tea called maté, and eat armadillo for dinner.

Darwin finally reached the little settlement of Bahia Blanca. He hiked to the area where the *Beagle* would meet him. There, he found many ostriches, deer, and armadillos wandering the dry landscape.

While waiting for the *Beagle* to arrive, Charles explored the area nearby. About 25 miles from Bahia Blanca he came to a stony beach named Punta Alta. Charles had heard that that was a good place to find the remains of long-dead animals. So he decided to take a look. The local people found this quite odd. Some even thought Charles was some sort of spy—walking around looking at everything, digging in the ground and packing all sorts of weird things into metal cans and sacks he carried with him. But Charles knew that what he found at Punta Alta could be quite important.

He wandered around for a while. Finally, he made

Toxodon Skull

TIERRA DEL FUEGO

a big discovery. In the muddy banks 15–20 feet above the sea, he spent hours digging. Carefully, he removed some bones he found sticking out of the mud. What had Charles dug up? It turned out to be the skull of a toxodon. The toxodon is extinct but it looked something like the South American capybara, the world's largest rodent.

The capybara measures about two feet in height and four feet in length. But the ancient toxodon was as big as an elephant. Darwin found it strange that they should look so similar, but be so different in size. Darwin found another bone of an extinct animal called the megatherium. The megatherium looked a little like today's slow-moving, leaf-eating sloth. But it was also much larger. The sloth stood just three feet high. The megatherium, at full height, could be twenty feet tall.

Charles's find stirred up more questions in his mind. The toxodon was like the capybara. Both animals lived in the same area, but at different times in earth's history. Why was the toxodon so much like the capybara, only larger? Obviously, the toxodon had disappeared. It was extinct. But if all species of living animals were the same ones that were created in the beginning, how could any animal become extinct? And where did the capybara come from? There was no evidence of it when the toxodon was alive. Was there some connection between the ancient toxodon and the modern capybara? This was a question to be answered much later.

In the meantime, Charles explored the geology along the way as well. He looked for proof that some great catastrophe had formed the landscape. He didn't find any. When he looked at the structure of the rocks, he came up with a different idea. What he saw made him think that perhaps all of central Argentina, or Patagonia, had once been under the sea. It had risen slowly to become dry land. This was an important idea—and a new one. It was very different from what most scientists believed about the earth's development.

Along the way, Charles kept finding specimens. Each one stirred even more questions. He saw an animal called the guanaco. Actually a kind of llama, it looked like a camel. He found the skeleton of an extinct animal called the macrauchenia (mah-craw-KAY-nee-a). He discovered it in the same area as the guanaco herds. Again, Charles wondered. Why were such similar creatures living in the same place, but at different times? Charles scribbled notes on what he was seeing. He would try to make sense out of it later.

Thirteen days after he left the *Beagle* at the mouth of the Rio Negro, Darwin met the ship again. A week later, the *Beagle* sailed to the Rio de la Plata, but without Charles. He had decided to walk the four hundred miles from Bahia Blanca and meet the *Beagle* at Montevideo. He hired a gaucho and a guide and started out on September 8, 1833.

On the trip, he and his guide hunted their own food—usually ostrich, armadillo, and deer. They often spent the night at *postas*, or crude outposts at which a couple of soldiers stood guard against the wild frontier.

Darwin reached Buenos Aires on September 20, 1833. He learned that the *Beagle* would not arrive there for at least two months. So, he decided to take a trip up the nearby Parana River. He had heard that there were fossils in the Santa Fe area. So he headed there—three hundred miles up the river. He trekked through the muddy roads of the backcountry and found fossils of animals like the toxodon, that he had already collected. He also found the bones of a mastodon, an extinct relative of the elephant.

By mid-October, Charles had become ill. He wasn't well enough to make the trip back by foot or horse. So he decided to ride down the river to Buenos Aires by boat.

Charles reached the area outside Buenos Aires on October 20. There had just been a revolt. All ports, including Buenos Aires, were blocked. No one was allowed to enter or leave the city. Charles was worried. If he didn't appear by a certain time, the *Beagle* might sail without him. But the *Beagle* would be anchored across the Rio de la Plata at Montevideo, Uruguay. He had to get into Buenos Aires, get on a boat, and cross the river to meet the *Beagle.*

When Charles got off the boat that brought him down the Parana River, he was captured by a group of soldiers. He talked to the commander, and explained his problem. The commander allowed Charles to see the rebel general, who controlled the troops at the entrance to Buenos Aires.

The next morning, Charles rode under guard to the rebel general's camp. He met the general's men, who looked to him like "great villains." He bargained with the rebels. He agreed to leave his guide and horse with them. Only then was Charles given permission to enter Buenos Aires.

Charles still could not get out of the city and he remained there for two weks. Finally, he escaped on a boat crossing the Rio de la Plata for Montevideo. With him, Charles carried cases of seeds, plants, insects, and birds to send back to England.

The *Beagle* was still not due to sail. So Charles went hiking into the backcountry of Uruguay. He found more fossils, and even bought the fossil head of a toxodon. When Charles returned to Montevideo, he mailed a crate to England. It contained two hundred skins of birds and small animals, as well as a number of the fossil bones he had found or bought.

The *Beagle* left the Rio de la Plata for the last time on December 6, 1833, and the *Beagle* sailed south along the coast of Argentina. It made several stops along the way. As the ship sailed on, Charles observed the sea and the landforms along the coast of Patagonia.

Most of Patagonia is a dry, grassy, windswept plain. Several rivers empty into the Atlantic at the coast and Charles often went with Captain Fitzroy and other *Beagle* crewmen to explore the land around them.

Darwin collected as much as he could of the wildlife of Patagonia—lizards, rodents, birds. He saw foxes and large herds of guanacos, one five hundred strong, on the plains. He also saw the tracks of pumas, or mountain lions, along the muddy river banks. But the hundreds of miles of Patagonia seemed monotonous.

> The [sameness] throughout Patagonia is one of [its] most striking characters. The level plains . . . support the same stunted and dwarf plants; and in the valleys the same thorn-bearing bushes grow. Everywhere we see the same birds and insects . . .

But Charles did find the time to think about some of the questions that had been raised by what he had seen. Darwin had found fossils of a number of huge extinct animals. So had others who had traveled in South America before him. It was obvious, Darwin wrote, that these extinct giants were very much like today's smaller animals. Why were they so similar? Could there be a link between the extinct species and today's animal life? The

Toxodon → Capybara

Megatherium → Sloth

Macrauchenia → Guanaco

During his travels Darwin found the bones of many extinct animals. He believed the animals on the left (ABOVE) were the ancestors of the animals on the right.

answer to that question was not yet known. But the fossils seemed to suggest that species could possibly change. Darwin didn't come to any conclusions about why they did. But he noted the "close relationship in form with extinct species."

CHAPTER SIX

Chile and Peru

From the coast of Argentina, the *Beagle* headed east into the Atlantic to chart the Falkland Islands. In mid-March of 1834, Darwin and several members of the *Beagle* crew spent a few days there. Darwin described the Falklands as "a desolate and wretched [country], everywhere covered by a peaty soil and wiry grass of one brown color . . ."

The islands were chilled and windy. Charles wrote that he often traveled and camped out there in a soaking rain. Still, he got the chance to see some of the animal life. Darwin found some animals like those on the Argentine mainland—but slightly different. Charles wondered why this was so, but he couldn't yet understand why. He stored the information away for later use.

One thing on Charles's mind was the next stop for the *Beagle*—Tierra del Fuego. The *Beagle* would pass that way again on the way to the Pacific coast of South America. Charles dreaded going back there, as everyone else did. He wrote:

I suppose we shall pay Tierra del Fuego another visit; but of this Good Lord deliver us: it is kept very secret lest the men desert; everyone so hates the confounded country.

In May of 1834, the *Beagle* made its way from the Falklands and entered the Strait of Magellan for the second time. This passage was worse than the first. The *Beagle* struggled through gigantic waves and shrieking winds. The ship and crew suffered for six weeks before leaving Tierra del Fuego behind, and sailing out into the Pacific Ocean.

On June 10, the *Beagle* began its northward journey along the western coast of Chile. Gradually the cold water, gray skies, and gloomy evergreen forests of the southern tip of South America began to vanish. The temperature rose and the skies became blue. Gloomy forest gave way to rounded hills, covered with low plants. By July 23, the *Beagle* anchored at Valparaiso, the main port of Chile.

Charles was delighted. He again sat down with his diary to put his thoughts on paper:

After Tierra del Fuego, the climate felt quite delicious— the atmosphere so dry and the heavens so clear and blue with the sun shining brightly, that all nature seemed sparkling with life. The view from the anchorage is very pretty. . . . In the northwesterly direction there are some fine glimpses of the Andes . . .

It was wonderful to leave the ship and step on solid land again. Mail from home awaited Charles at Valparaiso—as well as a new pair of boots. The *Beagle* would be in port for some time. So Charles moved into the house of an old school chum who lived in the city. But he wasn't content just to sit at home. Darwin wanted to explore and collect, as usual.

On August 14, Charles hired two guides and some mules. Then he headed out, through the foothills of the Andes mountains. Darwin headed north along the coast. The shore was very rocky and again, he found layers of seashells embedded in the rock. They were yards above the sea's surface. Charles could not help feeling excited. He was finding more and more proof that much dry land had once been underwater. Lyell's book kept coming back to him. The more he saw, the more Darwin believed that Lyell was exactly right. The earth's surface must have gone through many natural changes. But how did this happen?

Charles continued to climb and explore. He bought food and supplies as he went. Sometimes local ranchers would invite him for the night. Often though, he could camp out under the stars. He admired the planted fields and orchards in some of the interior valleys. After exploring the coast, Charles went inland and climbed Bell Mountain, 26 miles from Valparaiso. He wrote of his happiness in his diary:

> The setting of the sun was glorious, the valleys being black, whilst the snowy peaks of the Andes yet retained a ruby tint. When it was dark we made a fire . . . fried our charqui [dried beef], took our maté [tea], and were quite comfortable. There is an inexpressible charm in thus living in the open air . . .

After a visit to a copper mine, Darwin rode to the

Chilean capital of Santiago. By mid-November, Darwin had left the foothills of the Andes. The *Beagle* then headed south again to map the southern coast of Chile, the island of Chiloe and the Chonos Islands, off the southern Chilean coast.

Charles never forgot the thick, dark woods and the low skies which were almost always gloomy. Every day, strong winds and rain beat against the ship. Charles left the *Beagle* again on Chiloe, an island near the Chilean coast. Darwin had never seen a place where so much rain fell. It was always cloudy and the constant mist made it nearly impossible to see the nearby mountains. Charles crossed the island on foot. He saw that its people were very poor. They lived in rough houses and had only the poorest food and clothing.

"On the 20th of December we bade farewell to the south, and with a fair wind turned the ship's head northward," Charles wrote in his diary. Not a moment too soon, as far as he was concerned. The *Beagle* pulled in at a number of little coves as it went. This gave Darwin a chance to clamber over the wooded hills and cliffs along the coast.

On the night of January 19, 1835, Darwin and the crew of the *Beagle* saw the eruption of the volcano Osorno in the distant mountains. Darwin later learned that other volcanoes hundreds of miles away had erupted that same night. An earthquake had occurred at nearly the same time. That earthquake was felt throughout one thousand miles of territory.

All of this activity had taken place in the same chain

of mountains. Darwin thought that a group of volcanic eruptions and earthquakes occurring at the same time must have some connection. He thought back to the seashells he had found high above sea level. He thought of the plains of Patagonia that he thought had once been sea bottom. Could the same forces that caused the volcanic eruptions and earthquakes have also caused the raising of parts of the earth's surface out of the sea?

In February, Darwin experienced an earthquake himself. It was near Valdivia, Chile. He was exploring and collecting specimens there with his assistant, Sims Covington. While resting, they felt the ground shake beneath them. Charles and Sims quickly returned to the *Beagle*. The ship sailed north along the coast, reaching the port of Concepcion by March 4. Much of the destruction caused by the earthquake was plain to see. Again, Darwin wrote down his thoughts:

> The whole coast was strewn with timber and furniture as if a thousand ships had been wrecked. Besides chairs, tables, bookshelves, etc . . . there were several roofs of cottages which had [come off] almost whole . . . I observed rocks which, from the [shells sticking] to them, must recently have been lying in deep water, [and now] had been cast up high on the beach.

Darwin also described a tidal wave that had smashed through the bay at Concepcion soon after the earthquake had hit. The huge wave was twenty-three feet high. It wrecked buildings, uprooted trees and washed cattle from the fields into the sea. It even carried a boat from the harbor two hundred yards inland and left it in the ruins. Charles was seeing with his own eyes how the forces of the Earth could change the earth's surface.

On March 7, the *Beagle* set out from Concepcion for Valparaiso. The *Beagle* reached Valparaiso on the 11th. As usual, Charles wasted no time in arranging a trip for himself. On the 13th he set out through the Andes Mountains on a several-week journey.

As Darwin traveled, he often camped out in pastures, cooking his meals in an iron pot. He crossed rushing mountain streams and rode on muleback over steep mountain trails. Sometimes he would be lucky enough to get a room and meal at a farmhouse or village.

Charles again saw evidence that this high mountain area originally had been formed by the action of the sea. He wrote that the land had gradually risen. He had already seen sea-shells in cliffs several yards above sea level, in the Cape Verde Islands and on the Chilean coast. Now he was more amazed. Seashells stood in rocks now fourteen thousand feet above sea level in the Andes. Charles Lyell was definitely right!

High up in the mountains, Charles got wonderful views of the land below. He saw red snow for the first time. It had been colored red by tiny plants and animals. Charles camped out on some rocky ledges and in high, cold valleys. Darwin and his group crossed all the way to the eastern side of the Andes. There they could see the rolling hills and flat plains of Argentina stretching out in the distance.

On one night during this trip, Charles stayed in the small village of Luxan on the eastern side of the Andes. It was there that he was bitten by the Benchuga Bug. He wrote, "It is most disgusting to feel soft, wingless insects, about an inch long, crawling over one's body." This insect bite would become important in Charles's later life. He would grow very ill after his return to England. He would remain so ill, in fact, that he could seldom leave his home for the rest of his life. Some doctors think that Darwin had Chagas' Disease, which is caused by the bite of the Benchuga Bug.

Darwin and his party ended their eastward trip at Mendoza. Then they returned to the coast of Chile along the Upsallata pass through the Andes. This route was easier than the one they had taken on the way in.

The central Upsallata range of mountains is separated from the main Andes chain by a narrow valley. In this valley, Darwin found the stumps of petrified trees. These are ancient trees which had been buried long ago by mud deposits or volcanic ash. Minerals seeping into the ground with water soaked into the buried wood, turning it to stone over millions of years. The trees were many miles inland from the sea and thousands of feet above sea level. But Darwin knew by studying the land around the trees that this forest had once stood at the ocean's edge. The high mountains he was crossing were once the bed of the ocean!

In mid-April, Darwin returned to Valparaiso. But he was soon off on his own once again. On April 27, Darwin set out on a four hundred mile journey up the coast. This time, he took four horses and two mules. Captain Fitzroy agreed to pick him up again at Copiapo, in Peru. Charles rode north on horseback along the coast, cooking his own meals and sleeping in the open air. He noted the dry, barren climate and the geology along the way. One night Darwin was thrilled at his good fortune. He found a room to stay in—with no fleas.

By June 30, Darwin's trip to northern Chile and Peru was done. He met the *Beagle* at Copiapo. The ship anchored at Callao, a port near Lima, Peru, in July. It stayed there for six weeks, but Darwin did not take his usual long trek through the countryside. There was political trouble in the area and the government could not guarantee that Darwin would be safe if he left the area around his ship. Several different groups were fighting for control of the government. There were constant rumors of more violence. In fact, the president was captured by soldiers and shot sometime after the *Beagle* left Peru.

By this time, the crew of the *Beagle* had been at sea for nearly four years. There were letters from home at some of the larger ports. But the men missed their families and the comforts of home. Darwin could hardly remember the last time he had sat down to dinner with his family, or had walked in the gardens at Shrewsbury. Still, the *Beagle* had more than half the world to sail around.

Darwin had time to rest and think things over before the next part of the voyage. He had already seen and experienced so much. He had seen and collected many different species of plants and animals. He had seen evidence that earth's surface undergoes change. But many questions still needed answering. The next stop for the *Beagle* would be the Galápagos islands. Charles was not very excited about visiting these barren islands. But on the Galápagos, many of the pieces of his puzzle would begin to fit together.

CHAPTER SEVEN

The Galápagos, Pacific Islands and Home

The Galápagos are a chain of volcanic islands, six hundred miles west of the coast of Ecuador. Sailors on whaling ships crossing the Pacific would sometimes anchor at the islands. They would stop just long enough to take on fresh water, or to hunt the meat of the giant tortoises that lived there. Other than that, humans hardly ever came to these islands.

On September 17, 1835, the *Beagle* landed at Chatham Island, the largest in the Galápagos chain. Darwin wrote his first impressions:

> Nothing could be less inviting . . . A broken field of black lava is covered everywhere by stunted, sunburnt brushwood, which shows little signs of life. The dry and parched surface, being heated by the noonday sun [is] . . . like that from a stove . . .

As Charles and Fitzroy peered over the railing of the *Beagle* at the landscape, Fitzroy said, "Hell must be like this."

The islands are just south of the equator and are bathed in great heat. Jagged, black volcanic rock formed the island landscape. On shore, Darwin could see the island life—hundreds of large, black lizards scampering over the rocks.

The *Beagle* stayed at the Galápagos for more than a month. This gave Charles the chance to explore and camp out on most of the islands in the chain.

On Chatham, Darwin tried to collect plants. But in the scorching heat, he wrote: "I succeeded in getting very few [of the] wretched-looking little weeds."

Darwin was amazed time after time by the tameness of the animals. Birds didn't fly away when Charles got near them. He could come right up to one and even knock it over with a stick if he wished. Because the birds knew little of people, they had not learned to fear them. In his diary, Darwin wrote:

One day whilst lying down, a mocking thrush [landed] on the edge of a pitcher, made of a shell of a tortoise, which I held in my hand, and began very quietly to sip the water. It allowed me to lift it from the ground whilst seated [there].

Even more amazing were some of the strange animals themselves. There were wild pigs and goats in the scraggly bush on some of the islands. The tortoises on

61

the island had shells three feet in diameter and each weighed up to five hundred pounds. It could take as many as six men to lift one of them. Charles played with them often to learn their habits. "I frequently got on their backs, and then giving a few raps on their shells, they would rise up and walk away; but I found it very difficult to keep my balance."

Darwin watched the lizards there, too. He found both sea and land lizards. The sea lizards he described as "hideous-looking creatures of a dirty black colour." They were about three feet long and were usually seen sunning themselves on rocks along the shore.

The land lizards were slightly smaller, without webbed feet. They were yellowish-orange underneath and brownish-red on top. He tried experiments with them, too. He would pull on their tails, for instance, to see their reactions. The lizards would usually stop what they were doing and stare at Darwin. They seemed to be asking him with their looks, "Why did you pull my tail?"

Darwin was excited by the strangeness of the Galápagos creatures. But a Mr. Lawson, the vice governor of the islands, told Darwin something he found even stranger. Lawson said that even animals of the same species varied from island to island. The shells of the tortoises, for example, differed in size, shape and markings, depending on the island. Lawson said he could tell the home island of a tortoise by looking at its shell. Those from Hood Island had shells that were thick and turned up in front. Those from James Island had rounder and blacker shells. Their meat was also better to eat when cooked. But Darwin wondered why the tortoises on different islands would also have different shells.

Darwin later found that the marine lizards and the Galápagos finches differed from island to island, too. These little islands were no more than sixty miles apart. But they were home to 13 different species of finches. Each bird had a different kind of beak. The beaks differed in size and shape. Again, Darwin wondered why.

Darwin later wrote that the landscape of Cape Verde Islands and the Galápagos looked a lot alike. Yet the animals on the two island groups were totally different. The animals of the Cape Verde Islands looked like those of nearby Africa, as the animals of the Galápagos resembled those of South America.

After a little more than a month, the *Beagle* left the Galápagos islands. On October 20, the ship headed west across the Pacific to Tahiti. Darwin wanted to stay longer

Galápagos Finches

Small Tree Finch

Medium Tree Finch

Large Tree Finch

Mangrove Finch

Woodpecker Finch

Small Ground Finch

Medium Ground Finch

Large Ground Finch

Vegetarian Tree Finch

Cactus Finch

Large Cactus Finch

Warbler Finch

Sharp-Beaked Ground Finch

Darwin found that the beaks of Galápagos finches varied from island to island. Thirteen distinct species exist on the islands.

to study the strange animals on the Galápagos islands. But he had to be content to go over his notes and study the many specimens he had brought on board.

As the *Beagle* crossed the Pacific, Darwin thought about what a puzzle the Galápagos islands had been. The animals there were very much like those on the mainland of South America—with some small differences. Charles asked himself why. Had the animals of the Galápagos originally come from South America? Had they changed once they had lived on the Galápagos? He felt that they had. But how did these changes come about? What could have caused them?

Darwin's ideas were forming. They told him that species could change. That isn't what most scientists of his day were saying. And after all, who was he to disagree with them? Also, these new ideas went totally against his religious teaching. But Charles could not deny the proof he was seeing in his travels. These were troubling thoughts, but thoughts that he would keep to himself for now.

In November 1835, the ship stopped for ten days at Tahiti. Darwin used the opportunity to explore, as he always did. He took a three-day hike into the island's Central Mountains. He ate roasted bananas and cooled his thirst under the burning sun with sweet coconut milk and fresh pineapple. He climbed the mountains in the center of the island, following narrow paths through tangled jungles of fern and palm. Darwin said that the forests of Tahiti were pretty, but not as beautiful or lush as the rain forests of Brazil.

By the end of November, the *Beagle* left Tahiti for New Zealand. The ship arrived there on December 21. Darwin had found the Tahitians pleasant and friendly. But he found the people of New Zealand fierce and disgusting.

Both their persons and houses are filthily dirty and offensive. The idea of washing either their bodies or their clothing never seems to enter their heads. . . .

Darwin was glad to be gone nine days later, and on the way to Sydney, Australia.

The *Beagle* docked in Australia in January of 1836. Darwin was impressed by some of its cities and the good roads. He found the trees "peculiar," pale green and with few leaves. He was most anxious to see kangaroos and rode many miles for the chance. Darwin found the climate healthy and the country well stocked with goods. But he thought the landscape was fairly ugly and uninteresting.

After some trips along the eastern coast of Australia, the *Beagle* pulled into Hobart Town in Tasmania, an island south of Australia. The ship stayed there a couple of days before landing at King George's Sound at the southwestern tip of Australia. "We stayed there eight days," Darwin wrote, "and we did not during the whole voyage pass a more dull and uninteresting time."

The *Beagle* left Australia on March 14. Upon leaving, Charles wrote:

Farewell Australia! . . . You are too great and ambitious

for affection, yet not great enough for respect. I leave your shores without sorrow or regret.

By April of 1836, the *Beagle* had reached the Cocos islands in the Indian Ocean. The gleaming white beaches and coral reefs were beautiful. Darwin wanted to look at the reefs up close. So one day he and Captain Fitzroy rowed out to get a better view. Darwin's study of the reefs further supported his idea that earth's surface changes slowly. In South America, the geology convinced him that sea bottom could rise and become dry land. The coral reefs convinced him that dry land could also sink into the sea.

For the next few months, the *Beagle* continued its slow, zigzag course back toward England. It made stops at Mauritius, St. Helena, and Ascension Islands, and the southern tip of Africa. Then the ship headed west across the Atlantic to stop once more on the coast of South America before returning to England.

By this time, Darwin couldn't wait to get home. He ached to see his home and family again after almost five long years.

Four years and nine months after starting the voyage, Darwin arrived back home in England—at last. On October 2, 1836, the *Beagle* landed at Falmouth. Charles took a train from Falmouth and arrived at Shrewsbury late that night. He didn't want to disturb his family at such a late hour. So he stayed the night at an inn. Early the next morning, he entered his house for the first time in five years, and surprised his family just as they were sitting down for breakfast.

There were squeals of delight and much hugging and backslapping. Five years had changed Charles's appearance. He was thinner and had grown heavy sideburns. Dr. Darwin looked at his son and exclaimed, "Why, the shape of his head is quite altered!"

The Darwins had a great time talking and laughing and catching up on news. Charles had many exciting stories to tell. He was finally home after his trip around the world. There had been many dangers. But he had seen many strange and wonderful things. He would not have traded this experience for anything.

Charles had also begun to turn over some new ideas in his mind. Now came the work of putting it all together. Finally the time had come to find out what all of these new ideas might mean.

CHAPTER EIGHT

Beginning to Put the Pieces Together

C harles never forgot that without his Uncle Josiah, he would never have gone on his round-the-world trip. So he went right over to his uncle's estate, Maer. While he was there, he got to see his favorite cousin, Emma Wedgwood. One day, she would become his wife.

Emma had a good sense of humor, and was very intelligent. She had even been a pupil of the famous pianist and composer Frédéric Chopin.

Still, Charles's most important task was his work. Now that he was home, there was little time for taking trips or visiting Emma. He had to start putting his specimen collections in order and writing about what he had learned on the trip.

Charles was now twenty-seven. He had been on his own for five years. He was not anxious to live under his father's rules again. He also felt that he could do his work better in a place of his own. In December of 1836, he settled, with Sims Covington, in Cambridge. They spent three months sorting and recording the rocks, plants, and animals that Darwin had sent John Henslow.

Darwin then took an apartment in London on Great Marlborough Street. It was near the apartment of his brother, Erasmus. Erasmus had finished medical school, but decided not to go into medical practice. Like Charles, he had been pushed into medicine, but really didn't want to become a doctor. He lived in London, enjoying the life of a wealthy young bachelor.

Erasmus had quite an active social life. When Charles wanted a break from work, he would go out in the evening with Erasmus and his friends. They often went to parties, social clubs, and the theater.

Charles Darwin was no longer just a wide-eyed young man who loved to collect things. He had decided during the trip that he would never go into the ministry. He had become a full-fledged naturalist, and that would be his career. His old friend and teacher John Henslow and the geologist Charles Lyell both knew about the work Darwin had done aboard the *Beagle*. They had seen many of the crates of samples that Charles had sent Henslow. Several other scientists had seen them—or at least had heard about them.

Charles Darwin had also written many letters to Henslow about his observations on plant and animal life. Henslow had shared the letters with other scientists, too.

Lyell himself had read some of Charles's reports from the *Beagle*. He had found them very interesting. Much of what Darwin had found supported Lyell's ideas about geology. Lyell had long talks with Darwin about what he had found when he returned. Through the talks, Lyell and Darwin became good friends.

Charles was slowly becoming well known. Other famous and well-known naturalists were impressed with his writings on plants and animals. They had also seen parts of his collections. They felt he showed real ability as a collector and naturalist.

About this time, Darwin started to publish what he had learned on the trip. He gave a speech on the rhea, a South American ostrich, at the Royal Zoological Society. He gave another speech at the Geological Society. He spoke about Chile's volcanoes, and how they helped change the land surface along its coast.

Henslow and Lyell started to promote Darwin's work with other scientists. Darwin was too shy to do it himself. Scientists in several fields helped Darwin publish a five-volume report about the animal life he had found on his journey. The books came out once a year, between 1834 and 1843. Darwin edited them. The set was called *Zoology of The Voyage of the Beagle*.

By 1839, Darwin had also finished work on another book. It was based on the many diaries and notebooks he kept during the trip. This books described his travels around the world, including the plants, animals and people he had seen. The full title of the book was *Journal of Researches into the Geology and Natural History of the Various Countries Visited by HMS Beagle*. Later, he changed it and published it again in 1845 as *The Voyage of the Beagle*. "If I live to be eighty I shall not cease to marvel at finding myself an author," Darwin wrote when the book was published.

Darwin was not only a great collector. He was also a fantastic observer. The book gave readers a lively look at faraway places that most could never hope to visit themselves. It is still an interesting book today. In Darwin's day, it also gave scientists a look at new species of South America and the Pacific.

Charles Darwin had always worked hard at what pleased him—studying nature. Now it was all starting to pay off. Because he had stuck with his interest in natural science, he had been able to take a trip around the world. From this voyage he had become a natural scientist. He was busy publishing his articles. He was giving speeches and enjoying the company of his friends.

Still, the puzzle of how plants and animals developed was not far from his thoughts. The trip had raised many questions in Darwin's mind. They all came back to him as he went over his notes to write his book on the voyage.

Most scientists believed that species, groups of like animals and plants, never change. But what about the fossils of extinct species? For Darwin had found many such fossils himself. Didn't the fossils prove that certain animals—different from those then known—had once lived and died out? Didn't that mean species did change?

Some of these extinct animals looked like modern ones. Why was this? He was sure some change had occurred.

Darwin had also seen animals and plants on offshore

islands—the Galápagos, the Falklands, and the Cape Verdes—that were like those on the nearby mainland. But they showed differences as well. Was island life descended from the mainland life? Had they somehow changed during the time they were separated? How about the differences in kinds of animals like the tortoises and finches on the many Galápagos islands?

The Galápagos finches were an interesting example. Darwin remembered that there were about 13 different species of finches on the islands. Each one had a different kind of beak. The finches had probably come to the Galápagos from the mainland of South America long before. As they spread through different islands they had found slightly different environments and food supplies. In some places the birds' main foods were nuts and seeds. Birds there needed thick, strong beaks to crack them. Other finches had smaller, pointier beaks. Charles guessed that, where the finches had these beaks, they ate mostly insects. Over many years, birds with beaks best suited to an island's food survived best. So different kinds of finches developed on different islands to best eat the food there. This began to explain why a plant or animal might change—and how nature could cause that change.

Darwin also found differences in some South American ostriches. The ostriches looked slightly different as the landscape changed. The idea that species evolve, or change, little by little over time, seemed clear from all of these clues. But Charles wanted to know how it happened and why.

Darwin was not the first to suggest that earth's creatures had come to be what they were through change. His grandfather, Erasmus Darwin, had held such views. So had many others. But they could never come up with convincing arguments for how and why it happened. So scientists had never accepted the idea.

Charles tried out some of these ideas on his friends. Most of them said that they had no faith in his idea. But Charles had never been a person to take no for an answer—especially when his mind said "yes!" He had to gather more facts to prove his point.

The first step in proving that life forms, or species, changed was to find out *how* they changed. Darwin thought one key might be a process called selective breeding. Even in Darwin's day, people had learned to mate animals with certain desirable traits. That way, their offspring would have the same traits. For instance, if they wanted to breed a fast racehorse they would mate a fast male horse with a fast female horse. Hopefully, the animals would produce fast offspring. Then the fastest of these would be mated, and so on. After many generations, the breeder would end up with faster horses.

Darwin went to visit some of the horse breeders in England. They explained how they used selective breeding to get faster racers. It was used with cows, they told him, to get animals that gave more milk. Plants, too, were bred this way to get them to produce more food. Darwin finally understood how selective breeding was done by people to change species. But how was it done in nature without human help?

ENGLISH HORSE BREEDING

That piece of the puzzle began to fall into place in September of 1838. How? Darwin started to read a book by Thomas Malthus called *An Essay on the Principles of Population*. Malthus had some interesting views. He said the world's population was growing much faster than the world's supply of food. If everything remained the same, and every couple on earth had four children, the earth's population would double in one generation. In ten generations, or two hundred years, it would increase 572 times, and so on. This could spell disaster! The earth's food supply would never be able to feed the population. What could prevent this from happening? Natural and unnatural causes like disease, starvation, and war.

Darwin realized that life on earth was a great struggle. Most living things did not survive. Malthus showed him that life on earth would not be possible if that were not the case. For example, billions of plant seeds are

75

spread by the wind each year. Only a small number of them take root and grow into adult plants. If all of the seeds grew into plants, earth's surface would be choked with plant life. Darwin formed a new idea. He believed that nature weeds out creatures that are the least fit to survive, and saves those that are strongest. He called his idea natural selection.

Darwin had noticed that no matter where he went, or how harsh the climate, he had always found some kind of life perfectly suited to it. He also noticed that even among life of the same species, no two were exactly alike. All poodles, for example, have characteristics that make them all poodles. But even among poodles, each one is unique.

Perhaps the slight differences in individuals which come about by chance in nature give some creatures an advantage in survival over others. In a way, then, it can be said that nature selects those that are most fit to survive.

Thus it was with the Galápagos finches. On an island where insects were the main food, finches with long, thin beaks could catch more insects. They would survive better than finches with other types of beaks, because those finches wouldn't be able to catch as many insects. Then the long, pointy-beaked finches would have offspring who would also have long, pointy beaks. Fewer and fewer finches with other kinds of beaks survived and had young, and in time there were none at all.

Not everyone believed in natural selection. Charles Lyell was one who did not. He believed in geological change but not biological change. If God created each creature perfectly, any change would make creatures less able to survive. That, said Lyell, is why creatures do not change.

Lyell used the woodpecker as an example. Woodpeckers were perfectly suited to their environments. The woodpecker's beak was perfectly shaped to pick its insect food from the bark of trees. Its skull was made to withstand the stress of pounding. Its feet were made to grip the sides of trees as it pecked, with its toes turned backward to provide a brace. Any change would make the woodpecker less fit to survive.

On Charles Darwin's side, there was Lyell's argument that the earth undergoes change. He had seen proof of this on his trip. He thought of the chalky layer of sea creatures high up in a cliff overlooking the ocean. He also thought of the huge movements of the ground after the earthquake in Chile. If environments changed, then the life forms would have to change to survive too. So species that were once most fit would possibly be less fit in a new environment. If they did not change, they might die out.

In the 15 months after July 1837, Darwin reviewed his ideas and did more research. In that time he managed to work out most of the parts of his theory of evolution.

Darwin finally believed he had his theory, but he wasn't yet ready to let most people in on it. In 1842, he wrote a 35-page essay on it—and locked it away in a drawer in his study. In 1844, Darwin expanded his essay to 230 pages. But he still wasn't ready to go public. Dar-

Lyell's 'Woodpecker' Theory

the _beak_ is shaped to pick up insects from the bark of trees

the _skull_ can withstand the stress of pounding

two _toes_ turn backward to provide a firm foothold

Lyell believed that God created each creature perfectly, thus making evolution unnecessary. He used a woodpecker to illustrate his theory.

win knew it would shock people. Darwin believed in God, but his theory went against the story told by the Bible. Darwin feared people would say he was speaking against the word of God. He just wasn't ready to face the criticism that he knew would come from holding such "dangerous" ideas.

Darwin was a gentle man and while he was stubborn, he hated arguments. He also feared that his peers would make fun of him. Darwin felt he had to be completely sure of the facts before he could go public with his ideas about changing life forms, or evolution, and natural selection.

Between 1846 and 1854, Darwin did a huge study of tiny sea animals called barnacles. Barnacles filled the Darwin house! In fact, when one of his small sons went to visit a friend, the little boy asked his friend where *his* father kept the barnacles. By the end of the eight-year project, Darwin was quite tired of it himself. But it was useful. Darwin had no formal training in biology. Those eight years of studying barnacles was like taking a very long course in biology.

It would be nearly twenty years before Darwin would feel he was ready to reveal his ideas on evolution. But in the meantime, there was much more to do.

CHAPTER NINE

Family Life

By the time Darwin was in his late twenties, he was pleased with his success. He had an apartment in London, and lots of friends and activities to keep him busy. But he began to think that something was missing. He wondered if it was time to get married and start a family.

Always the scientist, Darwin made a scientific list of reasons for getting married and reasons against it. Some of Darwin's reasons for marriage were:

—Children (if it please God)
—A nice soft wife
—Constant companion

On the other side, he listed these points against marriage:

—Forced to visit relatives, and bend to every trifle
—Loss of time
—If many children, forced to earn one's bread
—Perhaps my wife won't like London

Charles thought long and hard about the good and bad

points. Then in the end, he wrote, "Marry, Marry, Marry."

There was little question about the woman Darwin would ask to marry him. He had known Emma Wedgwood, the youngest of his Uncle Josiah's children, since childhood. He was very fond of Emma. She was his first cousin, and they had always been friends. But as they grew older, the friendship grew into love. In Darwin's time, the marriage of cousins was not strange. So in the fall of 1838, Darwin went to Maer to ask her. But at the last minute, he lost his nerve. He began to think of all the reasons she might say no to him—he was not good looking enough for her, not interesting enough. Emma didn't like science and might interfere with his work. Darwin left Maer without asking Emma the question.

A few weeks later, Charles got up the nerve again. He wanted to marry Emma, so he would just ask her. If she didn't want him, he would just suffer the rejection and look elsewhere. On November 11, 1838, Charles finally asked Emma to marry him. She was thrilled. She had wanted to marry Charles for some time, but she didn't think he would ever get around to asking her. Of course, she said yes. Emma wrote of Charles:

He is the most open . . . man I ever saw, and every word expresses his real thoughts. He is particularly affectionate and very nice to his father and sisters, and perfectly sweet tempered, and possesses some minor qualities that add particularly to one's happiness—such as being humane to animals.

Emma Darwin

12 UPPER GOWER STREET

Charles and Emma were married on January 29, 1839, in an elaborate ceremony at Maer. The young couple rented a furnished house on Upper Gower Street in London. Charles jokingly called it "the Macaw cottage" because it had ugly bright green drapes and wallpaper that reminded Charles of the feathers of a Macaw parrot.

Both Charles and Emma had come from wealthy families. They had no money problems. Charles received a yearly income from his father of 13,000 pounds. The money Darwin earned from his books added to their income. Emma also had a large dowry—money given to her by her family when she was married. The couple started off with two maids, a cook, and a butler. During the first couple of years of marriage, they often entertained friends at their home. They also went out a lot together.

The Darwins didn't wait long to start their family.

The first of their ten children, William, was born in December 1839. The Darwins' second child, Annie, was born in 1841.

Charles's marriage did not interfere with his work in science. He belonged to several scientific societies. He continued to edit books and articles on the discoveries he had made during his voyage around the world. He was working on a book about how coral reefs were formed. He was also still making notes, thinking and reading. He wanted to solve the puzzling question: how did species develop and could they change?

All appeared to be going well, but a cloud hung over Charles and his health. Soon after he got married, Darwin came down with a more severe form of the mysterious illness that he had "caught" on his voyage. It would stay with him for almost the rest of his life.

Soon after Charles got back to England, he started feeling ill. He would get attacks of dizziness and stomach pains. His heart would race. Often, he could not sleep at night. As the months passed, he would lie awake, in pain, for hours at night. Any kind of excitement could bring on a new attack. Darwin had traveled around the world. He had hiked hundreds of miles. He had climbed mountains. Now, suddenly, he would become exhausted after just a short walk.

Darwin visited many doctors to find out what the problem was. They did all sorts of tests. They could not figure it out. In South America, Charles had been bitten by the Benchuga Bug. This may have given him Chagas'

Disease. Darwin showed many of the symptoms. But no one is sure if that is what he really had.

The Darwins moved from London in September 1842. They were tired of the crowds in the city of London. Also, Charles was often in poor health. They hoped he would be more comfortable in the country. The new Darwin home was Down House in the village of Downe in Kent. Just sixteen miles from London, it was surrounded by land and greenery. Charles described it as ". . . a good, very ugly house with 18 acres . . ."

It was a large comfortable white house, with many windows, and surrounded by gardens. The house had three stories in places and the Darwins made several additions to it as their family grew.

The Darwins eventually had seven children living in the house, and they needed every bit of space. Darwin did go to London from time to time. He attended meetings with friends. He also took some short trips around England and Wales with his family. But there would never be another worldwide journey.

Darwin followed the same routine at his home almost every day. He would get up early. Then he would take a short walk in the garden. Next came breakfast. Charles would then work in his study from 8:00 to 9:00 A.M. This would usually tire him out a bit. So he would lie on the sofa and rest. Sometimes he would then look through his mail. Often Emma would read to him from a popular novel. Darwin said he didn't care which book Emma chose. It just had to have a pretty heroine and a happy ending.

From 10:30 A.M. to 12 noon, Darwin would get up and work some more. He would do experiments. He would study specimens. He would make notes. On some days, Charles would feel stronger. Next, he might take a midday walk around a nearby meadow. Then, he would return to the house to read his mail, to look at the paper or to write letters. On some days he would stop working at about 3:00 P.M. On others, Darwin would take another walk in the garden. This would give him time to look in on his plant experiments.

By late afternoon, it was time for the family. Charles would eat a light supper. In the evening he would play a couple of games of backgammon with Emma. He kept score for years. Later in life, he wrote a letter to a friend bragging, "Now the tally with my wife in backgammon stands thus: she, poor creature, has won only 2,490 games, whilst I have won, hurrah, hurrah, 2,795 games."

At other times Darwin would listen to his wife play the piano. He also liked to rest on the sofa and smoke cigarettes while one of his children read to him. Bedtime for Darwin was 10:00 P.M. each night. But because of his illness, he was often unable to sleep.

Charles loved to be surrounded by his children. And they loved him. But he was not a very strict father. There was much laughter and playfulness in the house, and Charles would join in the games when he could. It was very hard for him to be stern. He once entered a room and saw his son Leonard bouncing up and down on a chair. He said gently to his son, "Lenny, that's against all rules." His son quietly answered, "Then I think you had better go out of the room." Charles, with a smile, turned around and walked out, closing the door behind him.

Emma and Charles had a very good marriage. They were very close. Near the end of his life, Charles wrote in his autobiography:

> She has been my greatest blessing, and I can declare that in my whole life I have never heard her utter one word I would rather have been unsaid. . . . I do not believe she has ever missed an opportunity of doing a kind action to anyone near her. I marvel at my good fortune that she consented to be my wife . . .

Despite his illness, Darwin did not give up. He had his family for support. He also had a strong will. So he continued to work. He even found time to do some work for his community. He helped with charity events, was treasurer for a couple of clubs and even headed one of them for a time.

Although he could not travel often from his house, many of his scientist friends kept in touch by mail. Others, like Charles Lyell, Joseph Hooker (a botanist), and Thomas Huxley (a biologist) visited him at home in Downe.

Darwin had many accomplishments to his credit. But the theory of how living things change still tugged at him. It would take more time, but Darwin was moving closer to revealing his ideas about evolution. The result would rock the scientific world.

CHAPTER TEN

The Theory of Evolution

Darwin was still thinking about how species came to be. But he had other tasks to finish first. In 1842, the same year he moved from London to Downe, Darwin finished his book on coral reefs. His theory on how reefs form was accurate and is still respected today. In the same year, Darwin wrote a 35-page essay. He discussed his ideas about evolution through natural selection.

More geology books followed. In 1844, he wrote a book on the structure and formation of volcanic islands. In 1846, he wrote another about the geology of South America.

In 1848, Robert Chambers also published his book, *Vestiges of the Natural History of Creation*. Chambers made his own case for evolution. Many scientists noticed it— and disagreed. First of all, most scientists didn't believe in evolution. They said there was no proof that animals and plants could or did change. They also said it went against the writings of the Bible. Everything on earth was created by God in the very beginning, in an unchangeable form. Second, Chambers was not a scientist. He didn't do enough research. So his reasons for evolution were easily proven false by scientists with more knowledge of biology.

The book was a major scandal in England. But it was published anonymously. So people had a grand time trying to guess who wrote it. Some even thought Darwin might have written the book—to Darwin's horror.

Vestiges was badly written, but it did teach Darwin something. He would have to back up his theory with lots of proof and research before he could present it to the public. Many people already disagreed with the idea, especially since it seemed to go against the Bible.

At this time, Darwin's closest friend was a young botanist named Joseph Hooker. Darwin had met Hooker through the Lyell family in the summer of 1839. At that time, Hooker was just getting ready to go on a three-year voyage to Antarctica on the Erebus. He had read Darwin's writings about his voyage on the *Beagle*. When Hooker returned to England in 1842, he and Darwin became friends. Their friendship lasted their whole lives. Hooker was one of the few people that Darwin allowed to read his notes on evolution. Hooker agreed with some of Darwin's ideas. But he still wasn't convinced that animals and plants changed over time.

Charles came to his conclusion about evolution slowly. When he began his voyage on the *Beagle*, he did not believe in evolution. But the things he saw changed his mind. As the years passed, Darwin became more comfortable speaking to friends and other scientists about his ideas on natural selection and evolution. Lyell and Hooker

Alfred R. Wallace

DOWN HOUSE

encouraged Darwin to go further. They wanted him to write a book about it. His brother, Erasmus, also said that he should. They said that if he didn't do it, someone else would surely beat him to it.

Charles Darwin was convinced. He finally decided to write the book on evolution. But *Vestiges* still haunted him. Darwin knew that his theories were right. He just had to put them down on paper in the right way. If not, no one would believe them.

In 1856, 14 years after writing his first essay on his theory of evolution, Darwin finally started his book. He planned to write a huge book, with maybe as many as 650,000 words. It would take two years to complete and would be over five thousand pages long.

Darwin began to write in May 1856. By 1858, he had written ten chapters. Then, in June of 1858, his work stopped suddenly. Darwin had received a letter from Malaysia that stopped him cold. It was written by a thirty-five-year-old English naturalist named Alfred Russel Wallace. Darwin and Wallace had been writing to one another on and off for a few years. Wallace had become interested in evolution, and while he was exploring the East Indies, he had plenty of time to think about it. Now, Wallace had come up with his own theory about evolution.

With his letter, Wallace had sent Darwin an essay in which he outlined his ideas about evolution. Darwin was in shock. Wallace's ideas were almost exactly the same as his own! After the shock wore off, Darwin became upset. If he came out with his book then, Wallace might think he had stolen these ideas. On the other hand, Darwin had worked on his own theory of evolution for twenty years. How could he just hand over all the credit to Wallace?

Darwin wrote to his friends Lyell and Hooker for advice. He didn't know what to do. They told Darwin to quickly publish a short version of his book. That way he could beat Wallace and get the full credit. Darwin thought that would be very dishonest. He wrote in a letter:

> I should be extremely glad now to publish a sketch of my general views in about a dozen pages or so; but I cannot persuade myself that I can do so honourably. . . .
> I would far rather burn my whole book, than that he or any other man should think that I had behaved in a [mean] spirit.

This was not a happy time for Darwin. His youngest

son had just died of scarlet fever. His daughter, Henrietta, was ill with diphtheria. Darwin was also sick and in grief. As important as his work was, Darwin had much more important family matters on his mind. So he left it to Lyell and Hooker to decide what he should do.

They decided that Darwin and Wallace should both get credit for the theory. So they sent Charles's 1844 sketch and Wallace's 1858 essay to the Linnean Society, an organization of natural scientists. Both men got credit for their work. But the dates clearly showed that Darwin was first with the idea. Darwin and Wallace were both pleased with this.

Darwin expected lots of criticism when his paper was read at the meeting of the Linnean Society. But the criticism didn't come—at least not right away. The 32 scientists at the meeting listened silently as the paper was read. They needed time to think about new ideas such as this before they could decide how to react. During the next year, Darwin decided to quickly finish his book on the subject. That way, all his ideas about evolution through natural selection would be out. On November 24, 1859, Darwin's book, *On the Origin of Species by Means of Natural Selection, or the Preservation of Favoured Races in the Struggle for Life,* was published. The book became known as *On the Origin of Species.* It turned out to be one of the most important books ever written. It changed, forever, the way many people thought about life on earth.

CHAPTER ELEVEN

The Debate About Evolution and *On the Origin of Species*

Darwin worked on the book every day for thirteen months and ten days. When it was finished, *On the Origin of Species* was five hundred pages long. It became a quick best seller. Darwin himself called it "tough reading," but people rushed to get copies. In just one day, the first 1250 copies were sold out. More had to be printed.

What Darwin said was this: He did not deny that God created all life on earth. Darwin believed in God. But he saw plenty of proof that earth's plants and animals had not remained unchanged since Creation. Darwin said that earth's species had changed, or evolved, from other forms into their present form. This took millions of years to happen. And it happened through a process called natural selection.

Darwin knew that each species—each group of like

animals or plants—produces more offspring than can survive on the food and space in that environment. The competition to survive, even among individuals of the same animal or plant group, is great. Any advantage an individual can gain helps it beat out others for food or space. This makes that plant or animal more fit to survive.

Darwin also saw that nature provides some individuals of a group with just such advantages. There are natural differences among members of a group, or species, that help some individuals survive better than others. These stronger, more fit members of a species are more likely to survive and reproduce. They then pass these survival traits on to their offspring. Members of the group who don't have these advantages are less likely to survive and produce young, and eventually their kind dies out.

Over millions of years, the small differences add up. The form of a plant or animal species may change. Some less fit forms die out, but may be preserved as fossils. Perhaps similar species, somewhat changed in form, survive and live on. This could have been the case with animals such as the extinct toxodon, which was so similar to the still-living capybara.

Darwin also said that animals of the same scientific class who differ widely from each other—for instance the horse and the porpoise—may have body parts that are similar. "What can be more curious than," he wrote, "that the hand of a man, formed for grasping, that of a mole for digging, the leg of a horse, the paddle of the porpoise, and the wing of the bat, should all be constructed on the same pattern, and should include the same bones, in the same relative positions?" Darwin believed this meant that many of these animals had a common ancestor. He laid out an amazing, new idea here: that somehow these lower animals and human beings might be related.

Darwin sent some advance copies of the book to his friends and to other scientists. These were people whom he respected. He wanted very much for them to accept his theory. Among them were Joseph Hooker, his closest friend and the leading botanist in England, Charles Lyell, England's leading geologist, and Thomas Huxley, the nation's leading zoologist.

Hooker called the book "glorious." He had had many discussions about evolution with Darwin over the years. He thought that Charles's theory was true. However, he did not believe in natural selection as the *only* cause for evolutionary change.

Lyell said he was "enchanted" by the book. But Darwin's old friend could never quite make up his mind about evolution. He could accept it only if God, not natural selection, was the cause for evolution. Darwin said he had Lyell "nearly converted" but he never convinced him entirely.

Huxley, on the other hand, thought the book was great from start to finish. He was a complete convert. He told Darwin that he would even be ready to defend his theory for him, since Darwin could not, or would not, leave his house to do it.

Even some clergymen were convinced. The Reverend Charles Kingsley, the queen's chaplain, wrote in a letter that evolution did not deny the existence of God.

We know that God was so wise that he could make all things; but he is so much wiser even than that, that he can make all things make themselves.

Not everyone agreed, though. Darwin received much criticism, too. Eventually, the criticism outweighed the praise. Darwin's old friend and teacher, Adam Sedgwick, said that he greatly admired some parts of the book. But he called other parts "utterly false." He said they made him laugh until his sides ached. Natural selection, he declared, was nonsense. Dr. Samuel Wilberforce, the bishop of Oxford, said that Darwin's theory made people and vegetables cousins.

Book reviewers often trashed the book. Cartoons appeared in magazines and newspapers, portraying Darwin as part man, part ape. Because Darwin said that people and some animals like apes came from a common ancestor, he was called "the monkey man." Because his ideas were different than the exact word of the Bible, Darwin was also called "the most dangerous man in England." Many people attacked Darwin for religious reasons. Some scientists attacked Darwin only because they secretly admired his theory and were jealous of his work.

With every new argument, more copies of the book were sold. By the spring of 1860, the criticisms were beginning to really get to Darwin. More and more people were attacking him. Yet most of his friends and supporters had not yet gone to the public to defend him. Darwin did not doubt his theory. But he began to doubt that the public would ever truly accept it.

At the end of June 1860, there was to be a debate on Darwin's theory at the meeting of the British Association for the Advancement of Science (BAAS) at Oxford. Darwin hated arguments and public speaking. He didn't think he could bring himself to stand up in front of a hostile crowd and defend his theory. Besides, as usual, he was not well. Luckily for Darwin, his friends Huxley and Hooker were ready to fight his battle for him.

The meeting began on Thursday, June 28, 1860. Darwin's old friend and teacher, John Henslow, ran the meeting. Henslow didn't believe in evolution himself. But he thought that Darwin's ideas deserved at least a fair hearing.

Huxley and Hooker had also come to the meeting to make sure that Darwin's ideas were presented. But even before the day of the debate, all Huxley heard at the convention was anti-Darwinism. He decided that people were not really interested in a fair discussion of the facts. So he decided on the second day of the meeting, Friday, that he would leave. As he was walking through the streets of Oxford, he met Robert Chambers. Chambers had written *Vestiges of the Natural History of Creation*. He was a strong supporter of evolution. When Huxley told Chambers he was going to pack up and go home, Chambers convinced him to stay and fight.

On the third day of the meeting, a huge crowd gathered for the debate. The meeting had to be moved to the University Museum library because it would seat more people. Over seven hundred people crowded the hall. In the center of the room, a small group of clergymen sat

Thomas Huxley

BAAS MEETING GROUNDS

ready to cheer for Bishop Wilberforce. Wilberforce would make the main argument against evolution. Lining the window ledges were a group of women. In a far corner, a group of students had come, expecting to see an entertaining show. Darwin's supporters were a small group. Two of them, Huxley and Hooker, were on a platform with Bishop Wilberforce. The three would give the main arguments for and against the theory.

The session started with a dull, hour-long talk on the intellectual development of Europe. A second man started to speak afterward, but was hooted off of the stage. Why? Because of his heavy accent, he pronounced the word monkey as "mawnkey."

Finally, it was Bishop Wilberforce's turn to argue against Darwinism. The bishop had been helped by Robert Owen, the head of the paleontology department at Oxford University Museum. Owen gave Wilberforce all sorts of scientific arguments to use against Darwinism. He was a very good speaker, and at first seemed very sure of himself. Hooker wrote to Darwin to give him some of the details of what happened:

[Wilberforce] got up and spouted for half an hour with . . . ugliness and emptiness and unfairness. Huxley answered admirably and turned the tables, but he could not throw his voice over so large an assembly, nor command the audience; and he did not . . . put the matter in a form or way that carried the audience.

Hooker sat on the platform, angrily waiting his own turn to speak. Other speakers had their way in the meantime. One was Fitzroy, who was then an admiral. Fitzroy was upset that his old shipmate had come up with a theory that denied the word of the Bible.

Finally, as Hooker continued in his letter to Darwin, he got *his* chance against Wilberforce:

My blood boiled . . . There and then I smashed him amid rounds of applause. I hit him in the wind and then proceeded to demonstrate in a few words: (1) that he could never have read your book, and (2) that he was absolutely ignorant of the rudiments of Botanical Science. Sam was shut up—had not one word to say in reply, and the meeting was dissolved forthwith.

Hooker's news could not have come at a better time. The news cheered Darwin. After the words of Hooker

Bishop Wilberforce

"Is it through his grandfather or his grandmother that he claims descent from a monkey?"

and Huxley, Darwinism could no longer be laughed away. After all, some of the leading scientists in England had accepted and defended it. People had to at least read *On the Origin of Species* seriously. They had to give Darwin's arguments a chance. That is really all he ever wanted.

As the years passed, more and more people took Darwin's side. Some ministers even agreed that God could have created the world and its creatures through evolution. He might have planned earth's life so that the creatures he created long ago would evolve constantly and change form. This is basically what Darwin thought, too. Younger scientists with open minds began to accept these ideas. Within twenty years or so of *Origins*, the ideas that species never change was nearly dead. Some scientists were still, however, questioning natural selection.

It was certain that species change, but *how* was still the question. Some scientists came up with their own ideas that put Darwin's theory of natural selection in doubt. In 1867, a Scottish engineer, Fleeming Jenkin, came up with an idea that troubled Darwin. Jenkin stated that some animals could develop differences that made them better and stronger than others. But when those animals mated with others, their strengths might not show up in offspring. Over several generations, their strengths would just disappear.

Darwin had no answer for this puzzling idea. He tried to think of one. Perhaps an animal's sex cells contained tiny units. Each unit would represent a trait, or physical characteristic. That would include traits that appear at birth, as well as those that are acquired during an animal's lifetime. For example, a person that works out and builds up muscles would pass along that trait in his sex cells.

Darwin was totally wrong about this. Using his example, a bodybuilder's child would be born with big muscles. This just doesn't happen!

Darwin's natural selection theory *was* correct, but the explanation of *how* species change could not be understood until scientists began to understand genetics. Genetics is the study of how traits are passed by living things from one generation to the next.

That started in 1867, when a European monk named Gregor Mendel reported on his experiments with pea plants. His results showed how certain traits are passed from life forms to their offspring. This information would have been useful to Darwin. It would have proven, too, that plants and animals can and do pass along certain strengths as traits. These strengths can be passed even when they mate with partners without those traits. But Mendel's work in genetics was not widely known until after Darwin's death.

When scientists understood genetics, they learned about DNA. DNA is the part of each gene which passes traits from parents to offspring and controls how all living things develop. Finally, the mystery of how life forms get certain traits was solved. Genetics also showed that strengths could be passed on in the genes without being weakened in offspring.

Today, most scientists think that natural selection does play a part in the way a species changes over time. Genetics has shown how these changes happen and are passed along from one generation to the next.

CHAPTER TWELVE

The Descent of Man and Later Years

Darwin didn't stop with evolution. He always had new projects for himself. In May 1862, he published a study on orchids. It was called *On the Various Contrivances by Which British and Foreign Orchids are Fertilized by Insects.* Darwin was the first to state that orchids are not just beautiful to look at. He wrote that its flowers help the orchid plant reproduce. He showed that the flowers attract bees, which spread pollen from flower to flower. Without the help of the bees, the flowers couldn't reproduce.

Then, he began studies of climbing plants and insect-eating plants. He built a hothouse on his grounds so that he could grow and observe plants all year.

So far, Darwin had stayed away from *direct* comment on the development of human life. But without addressing this question, Darwin knew his work was not complete. So, he got ready for the next round of the fight.

In 1867, Darwin decided to speak out about the most important topic touched by his theory of evolution. That was the origin of human life. Scientists had always argued about the subject. Darwin, however, had said almost nothing about it in *On the Origin of Species*. The book had raised enough arguments without it.

Alfred Russel Wallace was still writing about evolution, too. In 1869, he published an article saying that natural selection could not explain the origin of human intelligence. Darwin disagreed with Wallace and some others who had been writing on the subject. He decided to write another book to set the record straight.

In 1871, Charles Darwin came out with *The Descent of Man*. It was supposed to continue the ideas in *On the Origin of Species*. But this book would discuss man's origins. In the book, Charles showed the close resemblance between man's body and that of other mammals. This was especially true of apes.

Darwin pointed out that the blood of apes is like that of man. Man can catch diseases from apes and some lower animals. People can infect these animals as well. Darwin also saw that human babies developed in the same way as those of other animals. He showed that the way that the human baby develops in its mother is close to how the ape embryo develops in its mother. At some stages, the two are exactly alike. Darwin didn't think that this was just chance.

Darwin also had ideas about parts of the human body that are only partly-developed. The last few sections, or vertebrae of the human spine are like the structure of an animal tail. In other animals, they would be a tail. Darwin felt that this proved something important about human

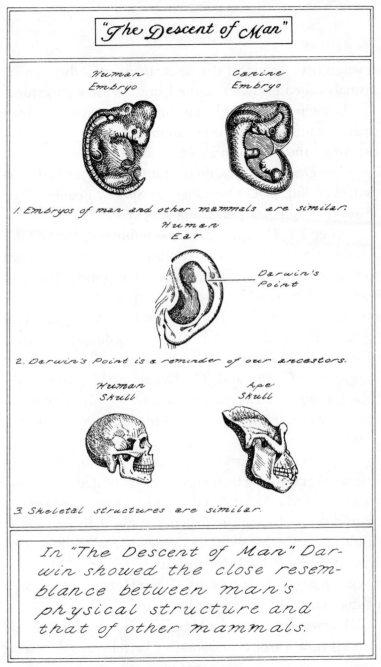

"The Descent of Man"

Human Embryo

Canine Embryo

1. Embryos of man and other mammals are similar.

Human Ear

Darwin's Point

2. Darwin's Point is a reminder of our ancestors.

Human Skull

Ape Skull

3. Skeletal structures are similar.

In "The Descent of Man" Darwin showed the close resemblance between man's physical structure and that of other mammals.

development. It meant that apes, man, and other similar animals called primates, came from the same ancestor.

Darwin also brought up the fact that apes and man share certain traits with other animals. He listed memory, curiosity, and boredom as a few examples.

The Descent of Man didn't cause the anger and misunderstanding of *On the Origin of Species*. People talked about the book without being shocked.

After *The Descent of Man* was published, Darwin decided that his great work on evolution was finished. Then something mysterious happened. The illness that had been with him since his voyage disappeared. Some people say that Darwin's illness might not have been caused by Chagas' Disease. They felt that it was due to the stress of working on evolution and keeping it all secret for so long. Once *Origins* and *The Descent of Man* were published, a great weight was lifted from Darwin's shoulders. His health returned as he shared his life's work with the public.

By this time, Darwin had become a famous and well-respected scientist. His books were translated into many languages and read around the world. He received honors from dozens of scientific societies in Great Britain and in other countries. He won the Copley Medal in 1864. This was the highest honor of the Royal Society. Dozens of scientists made the trip out to Down House for the honor of meeting with Darwin at his home.

Darwin had earned a lot of praise in his life and had also taken a lot of criticism. But he felt sure that what was in his own heart and mind was more important than what others said. He wrote:

> Whenever I have found out that I have blundered, or that my work has been imperfect, and when I have been contemptuously criticized, and even when I have been overpraised . . . it has been my greatest comfort to say hundreds of times to myself that I have worked as hard and as well as I could, and no man can do more than this. I remember when in Good Success Bay in Tierra del Fuego thinking that I could not employ my life better than in adding a little to Natural Science. This I have done to the best of my abilities, and critics may say what they like, but they cannot destroy this conviction.

From age sixty-nine until his death four years later, Darwin wrote three more books. He also wrote more than a dozen articles. The last article dealt with earthworms and how they changed the face of the earth.

Darwin's very last project was his autobiography. He never intended it for the public. He wrote it only for his children. He wrote in it: "With such modest abilities as I possess, it is truly surprising that I should have influenced to a considerable extent the belief of scientific men on some important points."

In Darwin's later years, his children were all grown and were making their own way in the world. They had always called him Papa. But as they got older, they told Darwin that they would begin to call him Father instead. Darwin hated the change. It was just more proof that his

Darwin - Age 60

THE SANDWALK

little ones were becoming adults. "I would sooner be called Dog," he said.

None of Darwin's children ever achieved the greatness of their father. Darwin remembered how difficult his father had made his early life. So he didn't push his children into careers. He gave them a lot of freedom to find their own way.

William, his oldest son, became a wealthy banker. His daughter Henrietta became Darwin's secretary and the editor of his written work. His son Horace became an engineer. George loved astronomy, and made that his career.

In December of 1881, Darwin had a mild heart attack on the front steps of a friend's London home. A few months later, in April of 1882, he had a more severe attack one night. On the afternoon of April 19, 1882, Darwin died at the age of seventy-three, with Emma at his side.

One week later, Charles Darwin was buried at West-minster Abbey in London, near Sir Isaac Newton. This was a great honor. Scientists from all over the world attended the funeral. Like them, Charles Darwin—the boy who hated school but loved to read nature books and collect—had become one of the world's great scientists.

Nearly 130 years after Darwin published his theory of evolution through natural selection, it is still a source of argument. Some people, called creationists, are fighting to keep Darwin's theory out of textbooks and science classrooms. They feel, just as many did in Darwin's day, that Darwin's theory denies the truth of the Bible and the work of God.

Darwin often said that evolution does *not* deny God. Evolution could very well be God's plan for the development of life after creation. Most scientists today agree with Darwin. Although evolution is still called a theory, it has a firm place in the way scientists think about the origin of life on earth.

Darwin himself was important for his determination and commitment. He had to bring together many facts to prove the theory of evolution. It is clear that he was a man who didn't give up on anything in which he strongly believed. He would be happy to know that today, evolution remains strong and generally accepted, despite all the attacks that have been made against it.

Anatomy
a branch of science which examines the parts of a plant or animal in order to discover what they do and how they work together.

Benchuga bug
a South American insect whose bite causes Chagas' disease. Darwin may have suffered from this illness.

Botany
the branch of science that studies plants.

Cambridge
world-famous university in England that Darwin attended.

Darwin, Emma Wedgwood
Charles Darwin's cousin whom he married after he returned from his voyage on the *Beagle*.

Darwin, Erasmus
Charles Darwin's grandfather. A doctor and famous poet, he was also an amateur scientist who thought about some of the questions about the origin of species that Darwin later answered with his theory of evolution.

Darwin, Robert
Charles Darwin's father, who was a doctor.

Environment
the objects and conditions which surround a living organism. In Darwin's theory, the environment that a

given plant or animal lives in, which includes the climate, plant life, availability of water, animal population, and so on, is what influences the evolution of that plant or animal.

Fitzroy, Robert
the captain of the *Beagle*.

Galápagos islands
a chain of volcanic islands located six hundred miles west of Ecuador. On these islands, Darwin made many of the observations of animals that later form the basis of his theories.

Gauchos
Argentinian cowboys.

Geology
the branch of science that studies the history of the earth as recorded in rock formations.

Henslow, John
Darwin's botany professor at Cambridge who encouraged him to pursue his interest in natural science.

HMS *Beagle*
the name of the ship that Charles Darwin traveled on in his journey around the world. He served as the ship's naturalist. (The initials "HMS" stand for "His Majesty's Ship.")

Hooker, Joseph
an English botanist who was a friend of Darwin, and who defended Darwin's theories to the public.

Huxley, Thomas
an English biologist who was a friend of Darwin, and who defended his theories.

Lyell, Charles
an English geologist whose ideas influenced Darwin. Lyell was the author of *Principles of Geology*.

Malthus, Thomas
an English economist whose theories about population growth influenced Darwin.

Natural science
the scientific study of natural objects. Darwin was interested in natural science as a child.

Naturalist
a student of natural science.

Natural selection
Darwin's theory that a natural process tends to cause the survival of individuals or groups best adjusted to their environment. His theory was not correct in certain ways because he was not familiar with principles of genetics which would be discovered later.

On the Origin of Species
Darwin's book, written in 1859, explaining his theory of evolution.

Patagonia
a large semi-desert region in the central region of Argentina.

Species
biological classification of animals and plants on the most specific level. Each individual in a species has common characteristics and general classifications. For example, a daffodil is one species of the general classification, flower. A cat is one species of mammal, and so on.

The Descent of Man
Darwin's book, written in 1871, that deals with the origins of man in terms of his theory of evolution.

Theory of evolution
Darwin's theory that species evolved or developed from preexisting types in response to their environment, or in order to be better suited to survive in their environment.

The Voyage of the Beagle
the title of the book which Darwin wrote about his journey around the world. The book is filled with his careful observations of plant and animal life.

Tierra del Fuego
island at the southern tip of South America. About half belongs to Chile and half to Argentina.

Toxodon
an extinct animal similar to the modern South American animal called the capybara. The discovery of a skull of a toxodon influenced Darwin to begin thinking about the origin of species and to formulate his famous theory.

Zoology
the branch of biology that studies animals.

1. What kind of student was Charles Darwin? Why was he the kind of student he was?
2. What is a species?
3. Charles Darwin liked to watch things carefully, and think about them. Why is this an important trait for a scientist to have?
4. From your reading of the book, what is a naturalist? Why is what they do important?
5. What did Charles Darwin's theory of evolution say? What evidence did Charles Darwin give in support of his theory? Why was this theory so controversial? Why is it controversial today?
6. What does it mean to say a species adapts to its environment? Give an example of an animal that is especially suited to live in the environment it lives in. Describe why.
7. Research who Thomas Malthus was. How did his ideas affect Darwin's thinking about evolution. What does the phrase "survival of the fittest" mean? Do you think it is an accurate description of life on this planet? Why or why not?
8. Describe what Charles Darwin said in the theory of natural selection. What were the problems with this theory?
9. Research Charles Lyell. How did his ideas about geology influence Charles Darwin?

10. Charles Darwin made many of the observations that led to this theory of evolution on the Galápagos islands off the coast of South America. Why were the animals on these islands particularly interesting to him? What did the differences between them and animals on the mainland of South America lead Darwin to conclude?

11. Research what is meant by "Social Darwinism." From your reading of the book, do you think Charles Darwin would have agreed or disagreed with the idea of "Social Darwinism?" Why?

12. What does Darwin's theory of evolution suggest about the relationship between animals and their environment?

Arnold, Caroline. *Genetics*. Franklin Watts, 1986.

Berger, Melvin. *Famous Men of Modern Biology*. Crowell, 1968.

Callahan, Phillip S. *The Evolution of Insects*. Holiday House, 1972.

Darwin, Charles Robert. *The Voyage of the Beagle*, abridged. Harper & Row, 1969.

Karp, Walter. *Charles Darwin and the Origin of Species*. American Heritage, 1968.

Klein, Aaron E. *Threads of Life: Genetics from Aristotle to DNA*. Natural History Press, 1970.

Miller, Jonathan and Van Loon, Borin. *Darwin for Beginners*. Pantheon Books, 1982.

Moore, Ruth. *Evolution*. Time-Life Books, 1968.

Settle, Mary Lee. *The Scopes Trial: The State of Tennessee v. John Thomas Scopes*. F. Watts, 1972.

Simpson, George Gaylord. *The Book of Darwin*. Washington Square Press, 1982.

Zappler, Lisabeth. *The World After the Dinosaurs: The Evolution of Mammals*. National History Press, 1970.

117